The University of North Carolina
Social Study Series

THE PLIGHT OF
CIGARETTE TOBACCO

THE UNIVERSITY OF NORTH CAROLINA
SOCIAL STUDY SERIES

UNDER THE GENERAL EDITORSHIP OF HOWARD W. ODUM. BOOKS MARKED WITH *
PUBLISHED IN COÖPERATION WITH THE INSTITUTE FOR RESEARCH IN SOCIAL SCIENCE.

BECKWITH: *Black Roadways: A study of Folk Life in Jamaica* $3.00
BRANSON: *Farm Life Abroad* 2.00
*BREARLEY: *Homicide in South Carolina* .... *In Preparation*
*BROWN: *Public Poor Relief in North Carolina* 2.00
*BROWN: *State Highway System of North Carolina* .... *In Preparation*
*BROWN: *State Movement in Railroad Development* 5.00
CARTER: *Social Theories of L. T. Hobhouse* 1.50
CROOK: *General Strike, The* 6.00
FLEMING: *Freedmen's Savings Bank, The* 2.00
GEE (ED.): *Country Life of The Nation, The* 2.50
*GREENE: *Constitutional Development in the South Atlantic States, 1776-1860* 4.00
GREENE: *Negro in Contemporary American Literature, The* 1.00
*GRISSOM: *Negro Sings a New Heaven, The* 3.00
HAR: *Social Laws* 4.00
*HEER: *Income and Wages in the South* 1.00
*HERRING: *History of the Textile Industry in the South* .... *In Preparation*
*HERRING: *Welfare Work in Mill Villages* 5.00
HOBBS: *North Carolina: Economic and Social* 3.50
*JOHNSON: *Folk Culture on Saint Helena Island* 3.00
*JOHNSON: *John Henry: Tracking Down a Negro Legend* 2.00
*JOHNSON: *Social History of the Sea Islands* 3.00
JORDAN: *Children's Interests in Reading* 1.50
KNIGHT: *Among the Danes* 2.50
LOU: *Juvenile Courts in the United States* 3.00
*METFESSEL: *Phonophotography in Folk Music* 3.00
MILLER: *Town and Country* 2.00
*MITCHELL: *William Gregg: Factory Master of the Old South* 3.00
*MURCHISON: *King Cotton is Sick* 2.00
NORTH: *Social Differentiation* 2.50
ODUM: *Approach to Public Welfare and Social Work, An* 1.50
ODUM: (ED.): *Southern Pioneers* 2.00
*ODUM and WILLARD: *Systems of Public Welfare* 2.00
*ODUM and JOHNSON: *Negro and His Songs, The* 3.00
*ODUM and JOHNSON: *Negro Workaday Songs* 3.00
POUND: *Law and Morals* 2.00
*PUCKETT: *Folk Beliefs of the Southern Negro* 5.00
*RHYNE: *Some Southern Cotton Mill Workers and Their Villages* 2.50
ROSS: *Roads to Social Peace* 1.50
SALE: *Tree Named John, The* 2.00
SCHWENNING (ED.): *Management Problems* 2.00
SHERRILL: *Criminal Procedure in North Carolina* 3.00
*STEINER and BROWN: *North Carolina Chain Gang, The* 2.00
*VANCE: *Human Factors in Cotton Culture* 3.00
*WAGER: *County Government and Administration in North Carolina* 5.00
WALKER: *Social Work and the Training of Social Workers* 2.00
WHITE: *Some Cycles of Cathay* 1.50
WILLEY: *Country Newspaper, The* 1.50
WINSTON: *Illiteracy in the United States* 3.50
*WOOFTER: *The Plight of Cigarette Tobacco* 1.00

THE PLIGHT OF CIGARETTE TOBACCO

BY

T. J. WOOFTER, Jr.
Institute for Research in Social Science
University of North Carolina

CHAPEL HILL
THE UNIVERSITY OF NORTH CAROLINA PRESS
1931

COPYRIGHT, 1931, BY
THE UNIVERSITY OF NORTH CAROLINA PRESS

THE PLIGHT OF CIGARETTE TOBACCO

PREFACE

THIS is a study of conditions which are extremely unfavorable to the farmer in marketing America's sixth most important crop, and of the economic forces which have created these conditions. It is an analysis of the factors which determine the price paid to farmers for leaf tobacco with special reference to the significance of these factors to a coöperative marketing program.

Throughout, these obstacles to the coöperative marketing of tobacco are presented as partial explanations of the failure of the former Tri-State Tobacco Growers' Coöperative Association. It should not be assumed, however, that they are insurmountable obstacles. They may be surmounted by a coöperative of a different type, and must be met if the marketing and production of tobacco are to be stabilized to such a degree that the farmers of the Southeast will continue to produce the crop.

From a theoretical standpoint this is an example of the action of farm price in a buyer's market, a market in which the buying is virtually monopolistic. The study also presents data as to the incidence of a sales tax on monopoly products and the reaction of price on farm production. It was felt that this analysis was worth while because so little has previously been written on tobacco in comparison with the volume of data on other crops and because of certain interesting peculiarities of the economics of tobacco.

Much vitriol has been spilled as to the low prices paid the farmer for tobacco, especially since, in certain sections, politicians who "save" the farmer are particularly alive to opportunities to declaim on raw tobacco price. This, however, is not an attempt to muckrake, since the parties involved seem to be acting in accord with principles which they think advantageous. But self-interests of diverse groups sometimes run counter to each other, in which case the most powerful group prevails and the interests of the weak are sacrificed. This, however, is to be expected in the present economic order.

This is one of the regional studies of social and economic conditions being made under the auspices of the Institute for Research in Social Science at the University of North Carolina. The author wishes to acknowledge especial indebtedness to Mr. Sidney D. Frissell, formerly an official of the Tri-State Tobacco Grower's Coöperative Association, for awakening an interest in this topic. Access to his files greatly facilitated data gathering. Assistance in data gathering was also afforded by Mr. Clifton J. Bradley. Especially valuable ideas on the tobacco tax were contributed by Dr. Clarence Heer. Acknowledgment is due the marketing and agricultural economics faculty of the North Carolina State College of Agriculture and Engineering for criticism of the manuscript. Collaboration with Mr. Frissell's work on the backgrounds of the Tri-State Association brought the realization that there were factors of production, consumption, and price of tobacco, the understanding of which is vital to a successful marketing program.

Accordingly statistical study of this field was undertaken. Though much laborious statistical analysis is back of some of these pages, the effort in presentation has been to let the statistics "show through" only so often as was necessary.

The method has been first, description of the factors in tobacco culture, the weak position of the farmer, the strong position of the manufacturer, and the auction market system which brings them together; then analysis and correlations of the time series representing the production, consumption, and price of flue-cured tobacco. As explained in the text, this particular type of tobacco was selected because tobacco types are so different that they act like different commodities, and flue-cured tobacco is the most important.

The source statistics on tobacco are contained in the current publications entitled "Stocks of Leaf Tobacco," formerly published by the Census Bureau, now by the United States Department of Agriculture, and in the *Yearbook* of the United States Department of Agriculture. A detailed discussion of the limitations of these data is given as an appendix. Suffice it to say here that the conclusions are usually based on such marked trends in the data that the margin of error in the original figures could be large and still not change the generalizations.

T. J. W., Jr.

Chapel Hill, N. C.
December, 1930.

CONTENTS

	PAGE
PREFACE	vii

CHAPTER I. TOBACCO AS A COMMODITY............... 3
Spread of Tobacco Culture—Importance of Crop—Localization and Uses of Types—Reasons for Study of Flue-Cured Tobacco—Findings.

CHAPTER II. THE CULTURE OF FLUE-CURED TOBACCO..... 13
Extent of Culture by Tenants and Negroes—Dependence on Credit—Relation of Yield to Cost and Value—Incomes of Tobacco Farmers—Summary.

CHAPTER III. THE STRONG POSITION OF
THE MANUFACTURERS............................. 26
History of the Industry—Dissolution of the Trust—Monopoly Practices Since Dissolution—Earnings.

CHAPTER IV. THE AUCTION MARKET SYSTEM........... 42
Procedure—Variations in Price—Collusion in Buying and Holding off the Market—Auction Marketing vs. Coöperative Marketing—Government Grading—Summary.

CHAPTER V. THE FEDERAL CIGARETTE TAX.............. 56
Amount—Changes in Rate—Incidence and Relation to Farm Price—Burden on Small Incomes—Proposed Adjustment for Farm Relief—Summary.

CHAPTER VI. CONSUMPTION AND FARM PRICE........... 67
Rapid Increase in Consumption—Leaf Used for Cigarettes and Farm Price—Disappearance and Price.

CHAPTER VII. PRODUCTION AND FARM PRICE............ 75
Stored Stocks—Trend of Production and Consumption—Areas of Increased Production—Changes in Farm Price and Production—Increase of Supply and Price.

CHAPTER VIII. SUMMARY............................. 88
Mutual Interests—Benefits of Coöperative Marketing—Difficulties of Coöperative Marketing.

APPENDIX A....................................... 96

THE PLIGHT OF
CIGARETTE TOBACCO

CHAPTER I

TOBACCO AS A COMMODITY

THE leafy weed which was used ceremonially by the Indians and made a fad in England by Sir Francis Drake has been grown in the upper South since the earliest colonial days and has been the main-stay cash crop of the farmers of large sections of Virginia, North Carolina, Tennessee, and Kentucky for more than two centuries. The Indians had been raising an inferior tobacco plant for years before the coming of white men, and the colonists at Jamestown began early to experiment with the plant. John Rolfe[1] first raised it in his garden in Jamestown in 1612, and by 1618 about 20,000 pounds of Virginia tobacco were sold in England.

SPREAD OF TOBACCO CULTURE

This $10,950 crop of 1618 became, in three hundred years (1918), a four hundred million dollar crop, and the estimated value of the 1929 crop at a depressed price was nearly three hundred million dollars,[2] and the value of the domestic manufactured products is over a billion dollars.

IMPORTANCE OF CROP

Tobacco occupies a relatively insignificant acreage in the United States, the largest area having been that of 1929 when a billion and a half pounds were produced on two million acres.[3] On the other hand it is a very significant crop

[1] *Three Centuries of Tobacco,* George K. Holmes, Yearbook U. S. Department of Agriculture, 1919, p. 151.
[2] *Crops and Markets,* December 1929, U. S. Department of Agriculture.
[3] As this goes to press the preliminary estimates for 1930 indicate a slightly larger crop.

from the point of view of its value. In value it is exceeded only by corn, wheat, oats, cotton, and hay. Potatoes and tobacco alternate in sixth place in value.

The per capita production of tobacco apparently declined from 11.1 pounds in 1793-1844 to 7.4 pounds in the decade following the Civil War. This tendency was reversed after 1875, and by the decade, 1895-1919, per capita production ranged from 10.6 to 13.7 pounds,[4] with still greater increase up to 1929. This reflects changing conditions,—the greater number of people, especially women, who smoke and also some increase in exports resulting from heavy expenditures for advertising at home and abroad.

Thus in several respects tobacco is of great importance to our national economy. It is one of the farmer's most valuable crops. It is one of the nation's most valuable exports and furnishes the raw materials for a very important industry, in which the net profits of the "big four" amount to over seventy-five million dollars annually. These products are now so universally used that their price constitutes an item in the budget of the richest and the poorest in the land. In the history of tobacco, a number of fortunes have been made by merchandizing, processing, and manufacturing, but very few have become wealthy by merely growing the crop.

The production of tobacco has been subject to the vicissitudes of agriculture in general and has had some troubles of its own. For instance it suffers heavily from excess production, and large production often results in poor quality. It requires heavy application of hand labor, and must be processed after harvesting so that its growers have marketing difficulties somewhat similar to those of the growers

[4] Holmes, *Three Centuries of Tobacco*, p. 154.

of truck crops. The tobacco farmers today are poor, disgruntled, and resentful. Their incomes are among the lowest farm incomes in the country and they are usually in debt to the supply merchant.

On the other hand the tobacco manufacturers are among the most prosperous concerns in the country. Their officials are high-salaried, and their stockholders not only receive fat dividends but they also participate in the increased equities resulting from the plowing of profits back into the industry.

This maladjustment of the conditions of the production of leaf tobacco and the manufacture of the finished product is the chief concern of this study. We shall, however, deal with only one type of tobacco,—bright flue-cured, which is largely used for cigarettes here and in the British Empire.

LOCALIZATION AND USE OF TYPES

The types of tobacco are so distinct in their trend, price, and manufacture as almost to be classed as separate commodities. The blended action of different soils, climates, and methods of cultivation produce leaves of different texture, color, and flavor. (See Map I.) These vary so widely that they are used for distinct purposes. Cigar wrappers are grown in Connecticut, Pennsylvania, South Georgia, and Florida. Cigar binders in Connecticut, New York, Pennsylvania, and Wisconsin. Cigar fillers in Ohio and New York. Louisiana produces a perique used largely for export. Upper Virginia produces a sun-cured tobacco which is processed in the open air after gathering. Middle Virginia grows a dark-fired tobacco which corresponds closely to the dark-fired product of Tennessee and Kentucky, some of which is used in the best smoking tobacco, and much of which is exported to France and Italy. Southern Virginia, North Carolina, South Carolina, and Georgia produce the bright flue-cured leaf which is the backbone of the British and American cigarette industry and which is blended in chew-

MAP I

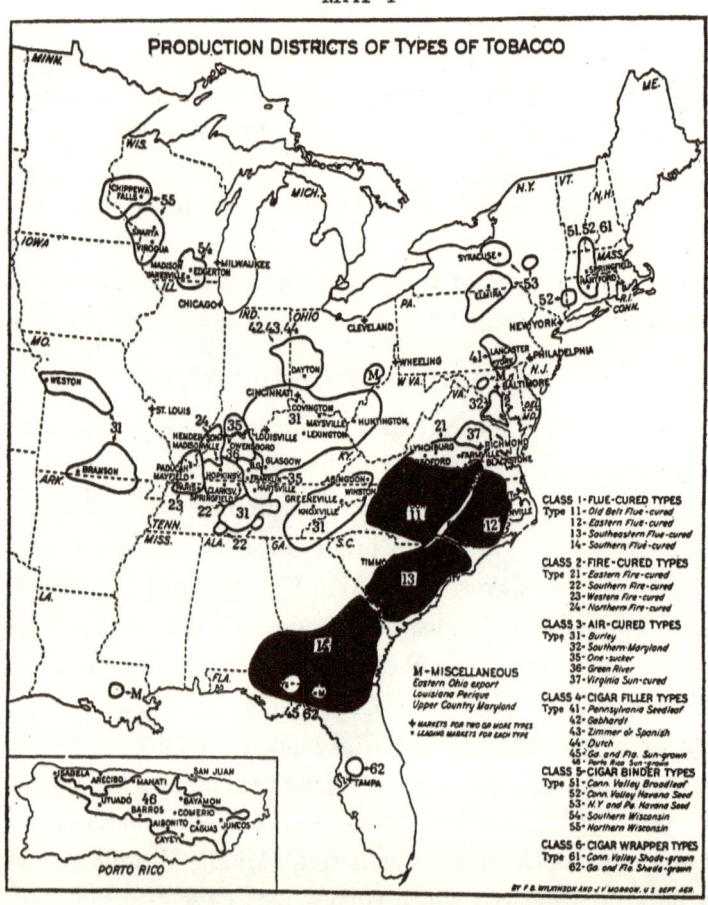

ing and smoking tobacco. Kentucky and Tennessee, in addition to their dark-fired tobacco, have long been famous for their burley which is the basis of pipe and chewing tobacco and which, of late, has been used to blend with the bright flue-cured in certain domestic cigarettes. Burley is also grown to some extent in Indiana, Ohio, and Missouri. Within these types there are grades classified as wrappers, leaf, cutters, lugs, and trash. Each grade is still further subdivided into numerous sub-grades of color and texture.

Each of the large tobacco companies has its own system of sub-grading designed to fit its own requirements for the particular blends which it manufactures. Also these blends change since each company has its experts and chemists who are constantly on the alert for new combinations to catch the public fancy. The exact nature of these blends have long been trade secrets of the companies, so that the farmer raises what his soil, climate, and weather chance to give him with little knowledge of what the demand or price may be.

This complicated usage of tobacco makes it necessary to discuss the commodity by types rather than as a whole, since not only do the conditions of production differ from section to section but the different types are manufactured in different factories, and the trends in demand for the manufactured products differ as customs of using tobacco change.

The more or less homogeneous bright flue-cured type, with which this study is concerned, is used for cigarettes, both in this country and abroad, and to some extent in smoking and chewing mixtures. It has been grown in southern Virginia and Piedmont North Carolina since about 1852, and of late the expansion in demand has created new bright tobacco areas in eastern North Carolina, South Carolina, and Georgia. The old belt of the Virginia and North Carolina Piedmont produces U. S. Type 11 flue-cured tobacco which is the foundation of the mixture used in making many brands of cigarettes. The new belt produces U. S. Type 12 and 13, in eastern North Carolina, 13 in South Carolina, and 14 in Georgia and Florida. There are slight differences in texture and flavor in these types but they all find their way in varying proportions (known only to the tobacco companies) into cigarette, smoking, and chewing mixtures.[5]

The relative production of flue-cured and other non-cigar types is shown in Table I and Diagram I. From this it will be observed that the flue-cured production is increasing more rapidly than other types. From about thirty per cent of the total non-cigar production, flue-cured has risen to over sixty per cent.

REASONS FOR STUDY OF FLUE-CURED TOBACCO

The choice of flue-cured tobacco for discussion was made for several reasons. It is the product of the oldest tobacco section. It is of prime importance to the cigarette and smoking tobacco industry in this country and in Great Britain, and for this reason its production has greatly increased while the production of other types has been stationary or has increased only a little.

The chief reason, however, for the concentration of this study on flue-cured tobacco, is the fact that in 1922 the growers of this type endeavored to form a coöperative marketing association which was one of the most ambitious efforts at coöperation, in point of membership, that has been attempted in this country. The disastrous failure of this association

[5] See shaded portion of Map I.

calls attention to certain peculiarities in the play of economic forces on tobacco. These need a thorough analysis before successful marketing reorganization can be evolved.

TABLE I
TOBACCO PRODUCTION (MILLION POUNDS)*

Year	Total chewing, smoking, snuff, and export	Flue-cured
1930	1327	800
1929	1457	751
1928	1207	741
1927	1072	716
1926	1153	564
1925	1180	576
1924	1071	437
1923	1321	593
1922	1072	409
1921	889	371
1920	1333	631
1919	1217	487
1918	1444	487
1917	1022	359
1916	919	263
1915	870	312
1914	805	275
1913	759	273

* *Stocks of Leaf Tobacco,* 1928, 1925, 1922, 1919, 1918, and U. S. Department of Agriculture, preliminary 1930 estimates.

Even now attempts are being made to reorganize the flue-cured tobacco farmers, because the recent price situation has been most unsatisfactory and because their appeals for relief from the Farm Board were met with the reply that the board only aids organizations. Whether a new flue-cured coöperative association, or series of local associations dealing with the product, will be successful will depend in a large measure upon the clarity of understanding of the peculiar economic conditions of tobacco and the ability of the organizers and managers to cope with these conditions. In passing it may be said that one of the fundamental causes of the failure of the Tri-State Tobacco Growers Coöperative Association was the relative lack of consideration for fundamental principles of economics as they apply to leaf tobacco. On the other hand the manufacturers, in their experience, have gained a familiarity with the peculiarities of the action of the supply, demand, and price of tobacco, and they shape their policies with these in view.

DIAGRAM I
PRODUCTION OF FLUE-CURED AND OF ALL NON-CIGAR TYPES

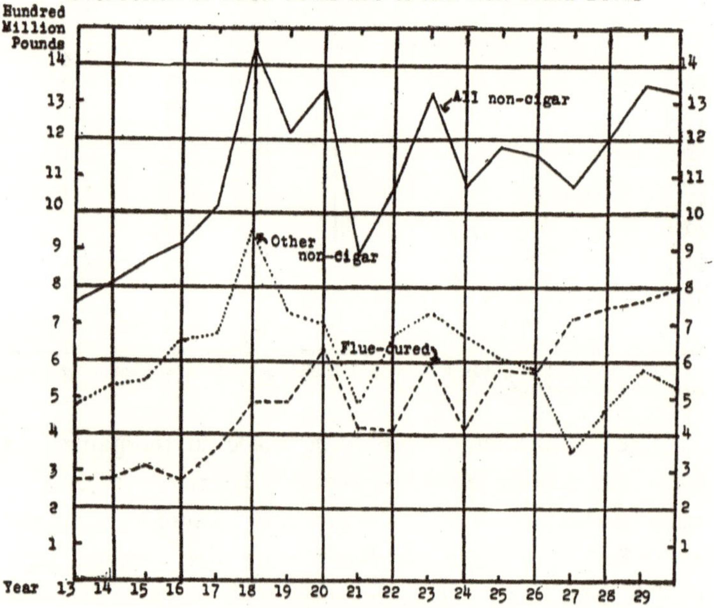

FINDINGS

To forecast what will be developed in detail in the succeeding chapters it may be said that the peculiarities of the flue-cured tobacco situation are chiefly the following:

(1) Cigarette tobacco for domestic consumption is eventually taken by four large buyers. While the efforts of the

Federal Trade Commission to uncover monopoly buying practices have been successful in some investigations and unsuccessful in others, the evidence developed shows beyond question that the tobacco companies understand one another very well and do not compete seriously in the purchase of the raw material. The tobacco exported likewise finds its way eventually to a few large English companies. The "big four" in this country and two large English companies take practically the entire output of flue-cured tobacco.

(2) These manufacturers have in storage an amount of tobacco equal to three years' domestic consumption and hence could go off the market for three years and still maintain their present output. This, together with the lack of serious competition between buyers, places the companies in an almost impregnable position for dictating farm prices.

(3) With such a small number of eventual purchasers there has been no demand for a tobacco exchange.

(4) The farmer is in a weak position because, while tobacco is eventually bought by few firms, it is produced by thousands of farmers, many of whom are tenant farmers who must market their crop when cured in order to pay their debts, many of whom are Negro farmers of no great acumen in dealing with the business side of farming.

(5) Tobacco must, within a few weeks of curing, be redried and carefully warehoused. This gives it some of the traits of a perishable truck crop. The redriers are expensive plants beyond the means of unorganized farmers and the redrying of small lots of tobacco is uneconomical. This is an additional weakness in the farmer's position in bargaining for a good price for his crop.

(6) The system of auctioning tobacco through warehouses has built up a vested interest in the warehouse system which is very resistant to any change in marketing practice.

(7) Tobacco production fluctuates violently with changes in price, so that any substantial advance in price merely brings thousands of additional acres into cultivation, causes the application of more fertilizer, and results in an excess production from which the tobacco companies increase their large stocks on hand at depressed prices.

(8) Manufactured tobacco is subject to a special internal revenue tax which amounts to a third of the retail selling prices in the case of cigarettes and which brings the Federal Government nearly an eighth of its total revenue.

(9) There is little correlation between current consumption and farm price but a close negative relationship between supply in sight and price.

CHAPTER II

THE CULTURE OF FLUE-CURED TOBACCO

THE area producing flue-cured tobacco extends from southern Virginia to the middle of the South Carolina Coast including a strip along the southern boundary of Virginia, all of North Carolina east of the mountains, and the north-eastern corner of South Carolina. In addition a non-contiguous group of counties in Georgia began, in 1918, to produce flue-cured tobacco. This area includes thousands of farmers who grow tobacco. In general the area is characterized, in Virginia and Piedmont Carolina, by small owner farmers or farmers with one or two tenants, and, in eastern North Carolina and South Carolina, by larger holdings cultivated by tenants and laborers.

EXTENT OF CULTURE BY TENANTS AND NEGROES

The production of such a large proportion of the tobacco crop by tenants is of especial importance in the marketing of the crop. The tenant usually has to have financial assistance from the landlord or the local bank in procuring his production credit. Notes or liens given for this purpose usually mature about the time the crop is marketed and are secured by the crop, and hence the tenant must sell in order to pay his debts. The tobacco farmer, especially the tenant is not a "live-at-home" farmer. He concentrates on the money crop to the neglect of the food and feed crops.

The percentage of farms operated by tenants is as follows:[1] Virginia, 25.6; North Carolina, 43.5; South Carolina, 64.5; Georgia, 66.6.

[1] U. S. Census of Agriculture, 1920, pp. 302-303.

It is significant that in eastern North Carolina, where there is the heaviest proportion of tenants, the coöperative association met with least success. There it had the greatest number of contract breakers and the smallest percentage of deliveries.[2]

It is also significant that a large proportion of the farms in the tobacco areas are operated by Negroes who are not well instructed as to the business side of farming and who are disadvantaged in their marketing operations. The following are the percentages of farms operated by Negroes: Virginia, 25.7; North Carolina, 28.3; South Carolina, 56.6; and Georgia, 41.9.

DEPENDENCE ON CREDIT

It is equally striking to see how great a proportion of the costs of farming consists of the costs of production credit. In a recent study by Roland B. Eutsler[3] the following facts as to 588 Negro farmers stand out.

PROPORTION OF FARMERS USING CREDIT AND COST OF CREDIT

Type of Credit	Percentage using credit	Cost of credit (per cent)
Short time cash	43.0	16.8
Fertilizer	65.5	37.2
Merchant	52.4	26.0

A study of white farmers in North Carolina showed slightly higher percentages using credit and a similar cost of merchant credit is against only 5.7 per cent for short time

[2] See unpublished study, Sydney D. Frissell, "The Agricultural Background of the Tri-State Tobacco Growers' Association."
[3] "Agricultural Credit and the Negro Farmer," *Social Forces*, VIII, 416-425; 565-573.

cash.[4] A very great proportion of the tobacco farmers are using production credit and paying stiff rates of interest. The high rate comes about from a spread between the cash price for produce and the credit price, and also because, while the credit is seldom used for the full year, a full year's interest is charged. The money is usually borrowed as needed during the growing season and repaid when the crop is harvested.

Such excessive costs of production credit eat viciously into the profits of the farmer. This phase of farm finance in the South is in a chaotic state. The credit is usually secured all from one source—merchant, banker, or landlord,—because the one security which can be offered is the crop; hence this security must cover all the farmers' credit requirements, and the creditor can dictate the marketing of the crop.

Thus, tobacco in eastern North Carolina, South Carolina, and Georgia is produced in a large measure by dependent tenants, many of whom are Negroes, who are in debt and forced to dump their product on the market when it is cured.

RELATION OF YIELD TO COST AND VALUE

"Tobacco is the most intensive annual farm crop grown on any considerable acreage."[5] Since the cost of man and horse labor is high, the acreage usually runs from four to five acres per farm. Its culture is intensive in the application of hand labor but not in the use of machinery and fertilizer. Application of fertilizer to the point of producing a rank or

[4] David L. Wickens and Garnet W. Forster, *Farm Credit in North Carolina: Its Cost, Risk and Management.* Agricultural Experiment Station, N. C. State College of Agriculture and Engineering, Raleigh, N. C., April, 1930 (Bulletin No. 270).
[5] U. S. Department of Agriculture *Yearbook,* 1922, p. 413.

bushy growth brings down the quality and hence the value per acre. The price varies so greatly between the grades of tobacco that the farmer gets his greatest return from a maximum yield of high grade tobacco rather than from the maximum total yield per acre. The yield and value per acre of tobacco in North Carolina are given in the following table:[6]

TABLE II
NORTH CAROLINA FLUE-CURED TOBACCO YIELD AND VALUE PER ACRE AND PRICES PAID BY FARMERS FOR THEIR PURCHASES
(1910-1924 = 100)

Year	Index Yield Per Acre	Ratio of value per acre to prices paid	Year	Index Yield Per Acre	Ratio of value per acre to prices paid
1929	99	85	1919	95	181
1928	104	99	1918	108	157
1927	110	117	1917	97	149
1926	105	130	1916	85	101
1925	102	108	1915	95	64
1924	86	106	1914	100	83
1923	108	119	1913	103	139
1922	77	112	1921	95	112
1921	86	105	1911	109	92
1920	107	96	1910	92	73

It will be observed from this table that the per acre value of tobacco is high.

The trend in the per acre value of flue-cured tobacco when expressed as a ratio to the prices paid by farmers[7] is slightly upward.[8] See Diagram II.

[6] North Carolina is used because this state produces only bright flue-cured tobacco. Virginia produces other types.
[7] Index of U. S. Department of Agriculture: Prices paid by farmers for articles which they buy. This is a national index. A more satisfactory procedure would be to relate the per acre value to a southern purchasing power index if such were available.
[8] Fitted through the average point and mid year as zero. The trend equation from 1910 to 1929 is $y = .89x$, 1918, 1919 and 1920 omitted.

The per acre yield showed a slightly upward trend from 1890 to 1910, probably owing to increased use of fertilizer, but the trend has been level since 1910.[9]

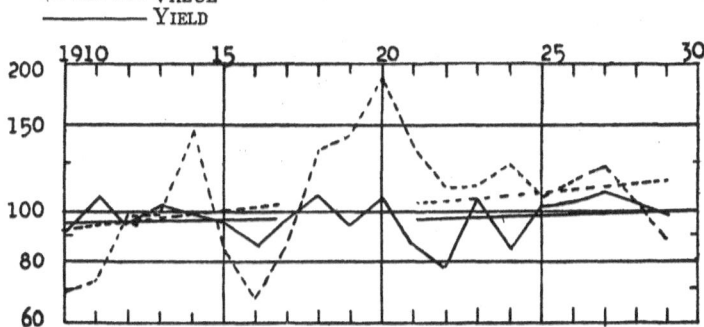

DIAGRAM II
INDEX OF YIELD PER ACRE AND VALUE PER ACRE, NORTH CAROLINA TOBACCO, 1910-1914 = 100%
(Straight lines are trends omitting war years)
------- VALUE
——— YIELD

The statistics as to the farm cost of production of tobacco are very inadequate. In fact the statisticians are not even agreed on all the items which should be included in the cost. The only material available is from scattered studies of the United States Department of Agriculture based on reports from the better farms. The North Carolina State average cost for 1928 was reported as $105.00 per acre as against a value of $133 per acre, leaving $28.00 net income from farm operations. However, the comparison of general state-wide averages is a very crude one.

In one of these studies made in Georgia in 1920 the cost of production varied from 44 cents to 13 cents per pound.[10] The variation in this cost is clearly associated with the dif-

[9] With the average point and mid year as the origin ($y = .31x$).
[10] U. S. Department of Agriculture *Yearbook*, 1922, p. 431 and 726. The prices given by the Department as of December 1.

ferential in yield per acre. The high cost (44 cents) was incurred when the yield per acre was about 375 pounds. The low cost (13 cents) was incurred with yields of about 850 pounds.

There are two factors in this yield increase: (1) The increased applications of labor and fertilizer which would increase the per acre cost; and (2) the adventitious forces of nature which might contribute to a higher yield with a uniform expenditure.

An increased yield may mean a lower cost per pound but, owing to the tendency of larger yields to be associated with poorer grades, the price per pound is likely also to drop with the increased yields. And hence the farmer may, and sometimes does, receive less for a large crop than he receives for a small one, and this offsets any economies gained by the larger yield.

This effect of yield on quality has not been sufficiently analyzed, but, with the establishment of a government system of grading tobacco, the way is now paved for such studies in the future.

This paradox gives rise to one of the most puzzling features of tobacco farming, namely how and when to fertilize the crop. Tobacco is produced on relatively poor land and some commercial fertilizer is necessary. In the flue-cured area "no system of rotation has been found which fully equals the simple expedient of allowing the soil to remain idle and undisturbed for a year or more with or without a covering of adventitious vegetation."[11] "The next best re-

---

[11] U. S. Department of Agriculture *Yearbook*, 1925, p. 57. Later experiments indicate better methods of rotation, but these are not generally followed.

sults are obtained with tobacco in continuous cultivation without the use of any soil improving crops."[12]

Under these circumstances commercial fertilizer is a necessity and, since tobacco is a high per acre value crop, the farmer can afford to buy fertilizer. He is in a quandary, however, in deciding whether to fertilize heavily for a high yield of low grade tobacco or lightly for a medium yield of high grade tobacco. An intelligent decision on this point would depend largely upon a knowledge of the character of the demand, i.e. which grades are needed to replenish the stocks of the manufacturers. Such knowledge is the very thing the farmer lacks. The manufacturers do not announce their requirements and the farmer is uninformed on the uses of the various grades and of the amounts of each in storage. Hence, he is completely at sea as to the kind and amount of tobacco he should endeavor to produce.

Here, quite aside from any effect of organization on price, is one of the fields of major usefulness of a large scale tobacco coöperative marketing association. One of its most useful functions would be the gathering of a body of information on the stocks on hand and consumption of the different grades of tobacco and the dissemination of this knowledge among the hundreds of thousands of individual small producers of tobacco.

Such a process would undoubtedly require time, and it is a much more deliberate program than the ambitions of the previously organized Tri-State Tobacco Growers' Association which were largely focused upon quick results.

However, even with this knowledge the farmer would

[12] *Ibid.*

still be able only within certain limits to produce according to the demand. He could select his lands, fertilize and cultivate as the situation seemed to require, but he would still be subject to the vicissitudes of the weather; and the quality of tobacco is often completely changed by a change in the moisture at critical periods, especially at harvesting and curing time.

The distribution of the cost of production of flue-cured tobacco by items is given in a study made by the Department

TABLE III
DISTRIBUTION OF COST ON PRODUCING ONE ACRE OF TOBACCO IN SOUTH CAROLINA CROP YEAR—1923
Summary of 47 Reports

Cost items	Cost of 557 acres	Cost per acre	Percentage of total costs
1. Burning and preparing plant bed	$1,105.00	$2.00	2.0
2. Fertilizer and seed for plant bed	520.00	.94	.9
3. Canvas for plant bed	519.00	.93	.9
4. Picking or weeding plant bed	394.00	.70	.7
5. Plowing tobacco land	1,689.00	3.00	3.0
6. Discing and harrowing land	559.00	1.00	1.0
7. Bedding or listing land	843.00	1.50	1.5
8. Fertilizer	9,294.00	16.70	16.6
9. Distributing fertilizer	436.00	.80	.8
10. Transplanting or setting plants	1,743.00	3.15	3.1
11. Re-planting and hoeing	1,113.00	2.00	2.0
12. Cultivating	2,264.00	4.05	4.0
13. Topping and suckering	2,363.00	4.25	4.2
14. Poison and applying poison for horn worms	893.00	1.60	1.6
15. Harvesting and housing	7,187.00	12.90	12.9
16. Curing	4,455.00	8.00	8.0
17. Sorting, tying, and preparing for market	8,636.00	15.50	15.4
18. Hauling to market	1,648.00	2.95	2.9
19. Rent of land and use of barns and sticks	7,860.00	14.10	14.2
20. All other costs not mentioned above	2,383.00	4.30	4.3
TOTAL COST	$55,904.00	$100.37	100.0

Area surveyed.......................... 557 acres
Total production on area surveyed........ 441,115 pounds
Average yield per acre.................... 792 pounds
Average cost to produce one acre.......... $100.37
Average cost to produce one pound........ .127

CULTURE OF FLUE-CURED TOBACCO

of Agriculture in South Carolina in 1923. The distribution of costs is given in Table III.

This indicates that a very considerable proportion of the costs are accounted for by the labor (about 80 per cent) either performed by the farmer and his family or hired. Thus tobacco cultivation is merely a device for the farmer to use his land and sell his labor rather cheaply and occasionally to make a small profit. When it is stated that the farmer loses money on his crop it does not generally mean that he sells for less than the cash invested in production but that he does not earn, for his labor, a wage equal to the usual level of farm wages.

INCOMES OF TOBACCO FARMERS

But tobacco is produced along with other crops, and its costs and profits cannot be strictly separated from the general farm operations. The growing of corn, for instance, is, in the South, largely incidental to the culture of cotton and tobacco. Very little is produced for sale. It is raised as food for the farmer's family and feed for the farm animals. A true picture of the financial status of tobacco farmers can, therefore, best be obtained from a survey of all their farm operations. Such a study was made in 1928 by the North Carolina Tax Commission covering representative farms in all sections of the state.[13]

In the Piedmont section, tobacco and a little cotton are grown on small owner operated farms. The net income in cash and in food consumed in this section, was just over $1,200. In the coast counties larger farms are operated and the proportions of tobacco and cotton are more nearly equal.

[13] Report of N. C. Tax Commission, 1928, pp. 120, 124.

TABLE IV
AVERAGE FARM INCOMES AND EXPENDITURES—NORTH CAROLINA, 1928

	Piedmont	Tidewater
Number of Farms	311	229
Capital	$6,810	$7,489
Land	3,961	4,620
Improvements	2,127	1,953
Livestock	351	463
Machinery	221	225
Feed	150	228
Acreage	109	150
Crops	32	41
Cleared pasture	6	3
Wood pasture	6	12
Woods	44	76
Other	21	18
Crop sales	970	1,662
Peanuts	0	368
Tobacco	642	214
Cotton and seed	191	327
Wheat	42	0
Corn	30	0
Truck crops	38	436
Other Crops	27	98
Irish potatoes	0	219
Livestock and product sales	209	282
Dairy products	101	58
Poultry and eggs	59	40
Hogs	28	161
Other	21	23
Wood lot product sales	11	12
Work off the form	63	48
Other	6	16
Total cash receipts	$1,259	$2,020
Inventory increases	68	107
Real estate	41	22
Livestock	14	24
Machinery	..	14
Feed	13	47
Family living from farm	567	430
Food	393	283
Wood	39	30
Use of house	135	117
Gross receipts	$1,894	$2,557
Gross expenses	679	1,316
Net income	$1,215	$1,241

CULTURE OF FLUE-CURED TOBACCO

The net income on these farms was about $1,250. The year (1927) when this study was made was one in which cotton conditions were about normal in relation to the past decade and tobacco conditions were slightly above normal.

The culture of tobacco requires much hard labor. It involves difficult and unpleasant tasks. In the early spring a seed bed is prepared in a sheltered position, sometimes in the woods. When the plants have gotten sturdy they are transplanted by hand to fields which have been prepared. A second transplanting is usually required to replace plants which have died. The crop has to be kept clean during the growing season; when it has attained the proper height it is "topped" to promote quality of the leaves on the lower portion of the plant. Poison has to be applied for the horn worm and wire worm or they must be picked off, and when the leaves have matured they are stripped from the plant by hand and carried to the "tobacco barn" or curing house.

Curing in the bright tobacco belt is accomplished in rectangular high barns under which the heat is carried in flues. These barns cost from $200 to $250 to build. They are of logs chinked with mud or cement, and the furnace is of rock with flues of galvanized iron. From one to ten barns are on each farm. This expense adds materially to the original capital necessary to start the cultivation of tobacco, and the necessity for careful curing adds materially to the requirement for skill in tobacco farming.

One feature of tobacco places it almost in the class of perishable crops and adds to the weakness of the bargaining position of the farmer. That is the necessity for redrying before it is stored. Within several weeks after the curing process the leaf has to be redried by steam to remove the surplus moisture. These redriers are expensive plants and are beyond the means of the individual farmer, hence they are in the hands of private corporations. This is one more reason why the farmer must sell his crop soon after curing it and cannot hold it at home as can the cotton farmer if he is not in debt.

When the farmer has cured his tobacco, he ties it in bunches called "hands" and separates trash, lugs, and leaf, and he knows in a general way that his leaf is good, medium, or poor, but exactly what grade he has or what the demand is for that grade he does not know. So, hoping for the best, but knowing that his debts must be paid from the crop, he heaps it high on his wagon, piles on tarpaulin or bed quilts for protection and goes to the auction sale.

Summary

Flue-cured tobacco is produced by thousands of farmers, many of whom are tenants and Negroes. They are in a weak marketing position because of debts maturing when the crop is cured. This weakness is accentuated by the fact that tobacco, to be held, must be redried soon after curing. While tobacco is a high per acre value crop, the costs, especially the labor costs, are also high, and these costs (per pound) tend, within limits, to fluctuate inversely with the yield per acre. Furthermore, the quality of the product, and hence the price, also varies inversely with the yield so that the farmer never knows exactly what he is producing, what the demand for his product is likely to be, or what his chances for profit are. With these handicaps and the tendency to over-produce, which will be discussed later, the farmer is in a very weak market position.

His returns from farming even in good years are low, averaging around $1,200 per family. This is from one-half to two-thirds of the return in other farming sections. In frequently recurring depressions he loses his surplus and is plunged into debt for which the interest charges are excessive.

CHAPTER III
THE STRONG POSITION OF THE MANUFACTURERS

THE manufacture of tobacco products has built an industry of tremendous proportions and a high degree of concentration. The manufacture of cigars is more scattered, but the domestic manufacture of cigarettes, pipe tobacco, and chewing tobacco is in the hands of the four successor companies which resulted from the dissolution of the "tobacco trust" in 1911.

Of their buying activities in the flue-cured area the Federal Trade Commission report of 1925 has the following to say:[1]

In the region most concerned in this inquiry we find demand for the types of tobacco grown in Virginia, North Carolina, and South Carolina characterized by the active buying of four large manufacturers in the domestic trade and two large export companies. These are the American Tobacco Co., P. Lorillard & Co., Liggett & Myers Tobacco Co., R. J. Reynolds Tobacco Co., the Export Leaf Tobacco Co. (the buying agency for the British-American Tobacco Co.), and the Imperial Tobacco Co., the latter two buying entirely for export. In addition to these competitive factors, there are in this region a large number of other regular buyers who purchase leaf tobacco as the agents for domestic and foreign manufacturers and who also buy and sell for their own account. This class of buyers, generally called dealers, purchases about 25 per cent of the total production in the three States. The combined purchases of the American Tobacco Co., and the Imperial Tobacco Co. of the types of tobacco grown in this region and handled by the (Tri-State) Tobacco Growers Coöperative Association are from 25 to 30 per cent of the total crop.

Thus twenty-five per cent is taken by dealers to be eventually repurchased by the big firms or by exporters, twenty-five to

[1] *The American Tobacco Company and the Imperial Tobacco Company*, Report of the Federal Trade Commission, 1926, p. 5.

STRONG POSITION OF MANUFACTURERS 27

30 per cent by the American and the Imperial Companies, and from forty-five to fifty per cent by the other three members of the "big four."

Such concentration of buying power is almost without parallel in any major industry of the country and, from 1890 to 1911, the period of the operation of the trust, the concentration was even greater as the field was preëmpted by the American Tobacco Company at home and the Imperial Tobacco Company in the export field. In order to divide the field these companies formed the British American Tobacco Company which looked after their common interests. In 1902 contracts were signed empowering the Imperial to manufacture the brands of the American in England and the American to manufacture the brands of the Imperial in America, and common purchasing agencies were frequently used.

HISTORY OF THE INDUSTRY

The following quotations from Boyd's *Story of Durham*[2] show the beginning of this industry and the factors which built it.

The development of the tobacco industry was by no means accidental. Conditions and events before 1865 prepared the way. From colonial days tobacco had been produced in North Carolina, but for a long time it was considered inferior to Virginia tobacco, and in Virginia also were all the large markets and the large factories. However, the year 1852 marked the beginning of a change. Eli and Elisha Slade of Caswell County, by chance, produced a fine yellow leaf. They believed this to be the result of curing with artificial heat, but experience soon demonstrated that the determining factor in producing the new type of weed was the land—a light, sandy, siliceous soil. Soon production spread into the adjoining counties of Person, Warren, Orange, Granville, and Rockingham. As the leaf produced

[2] *Story of Durham, City of the New South*, W. K. Boyd, Duke University Press, 1925, pp. 57-62, 67-68, 71, 75, 80-93.

was lighter in color than that raised further east, it was known as Bright Tobacco and the region which produced it the Bright Tobacco Belt. It was especially well adapted to smoking.

Manufacture soon followed. The farmers shredded the Bright Tobacco and then prepared it for smoking or chewing and peddled it throughout the state. With such a background manufacture was begun in Durham in 1858. In that year Robert F. Morris moved to the hamlet and with his sons opened a factory in a small house that stood somewhere on the land now occupied by the Bull Factory. These were the pioneer tobacconists of Durham. Soon they took a partner, W. A. Wright, of Virginia, and the firm name of Morris and Wright appeared. Mr. Wright invented a name for the product —"Best Flavored Spanish Smoking Tobacco"—adopted because of a flavoring mixture which he contributed to the business. . . . Just before the Civil War Mr. J. R. Green purchased the business.

What progress he made before the close of the war we do not know, but in 1865 a calamity overtook him which proved a blessing. The Confederate Army, as it fell back through Durham, made the acquaintance of Green's tobacco, and the Federals, who followed hard on their heels, raided the factory. Apparently Mr. Green was ruined; but so well did the soldiers appreciate the smoke from the Spanish Flavored Durham Tobacco that after their return to their homes orders began to pour in. Hence the business revived. . . .

Incidentally it might be mentioned that after each war cigarette smoking seems to have increased rapidly. But Mr. Green had grave problems. He needed a distinctive and protected trademark as he had many imitators, other cities adopting the word Durham for their product. This he solved by acting upon the suggestion of a friend and adopting the bull as an emblem. W. T. Blackwell succeeded J. R. Green and after extended litigations the trademark was protected.

Soon endorsements of the brand were secured. A gold medal and certificate of merit was awarded "Bull Durham" at the Philadelphia Centennial Exposition in 1876. Prominent men wrote letters to the company approving its product, and some of these were published. Among the notable smokers of the country who permitted their testimonials to be published were Senators Blackburn, of Kentucky,

Coke, of Texas, Butler, of South Carolina, Cockrell, of Missouri, and Harris, of Tennessee; Reverend W. H. Milburn, Chaplain of the United States Senate, and Alexander H. Stephens, former Vice-President of the Confederacy, also praised "Bull Durham." When Anne Trackeray called on Alfred Lord Tennyson, poet laureate of England, she found him peacefully smoking "Bull Durham" with which he had become acquainted through James Russell Lowell, the American poet and man of letters. Thomas Carlyle also used "Bull Durham." . . . But this was not all; premiums and prizes, ranging from razors to expensive mantel clocks were offered to the purchasers. And, finally, the Bull was painted on signs throughout the land. . . . The Old World was also invaded—not only Europe, but also the Orient—and the Bull was once to be seen on the pyramids of Egypt. . . .

The other innovation that was necessary for nation-wide and world-wide production of manufactured tobacco was the introduction of machinery. And here again the Bull excelled. In the early years of the industry the manufacturing methods were very simple. The leaf tobacco was placed on long tables, and Negro boys beat it with flails. It was then raked into sieves, and that which passed through was turned over to more skilled workers who weighed it and placed it in bags; the refuse was then re-sifted. This was evidently too slow and also too expensive a process for large scale production. The man who led the way in the solution of the problems was Julian S. Carr. While on a business trip to Richmond he learned that the Virginia manufacturers were using machinery behind locked doors. He secured the name and address of the maker of machines, and soon one of these, which shredded and ground the tobacco, was brought to the Bull Factory, and the public was given a demonstration. This was the Smith Machine, so-called from the inventor, H. M. Smith. In principle it was based on the wheat thresher. But the machine itself raised new problems. One was that of packing tobacco into bags, for the tobacco came out of the machine too rapidly for hand packing. This difficulty was overcome by L. W. Lawrence, who invented a machine which packed the bags. Another problem was that of the production of bags. . . .

The growth of the Bull Durham Company was rapid, but in its later days the management was not so aggressive and manufactured cigarettes began to cut into its sales, so the company was finally acquired by the American Tobacco Company.

The story of the growth of the American Tobacco Company from a log cabin 20 x 30 feet to the present proportions is a romance in itself.

In 1865 Washington Duke was forty-five years of age. A widower with children, he served for a while in the Confederate Army and was kept in a military prison a short while after the surrender.

He was soon discharged and sent to New Bern. From that place he walked home, a distance of 137 miles. He found that his farm of three hundred acres which he had acquired before the war by thrift and industry, had been raided by the Federal soldiers who had carried away practically all supplies. He was indeed destitute, having only fifty cents in good money, secured from a Federal soldier in exchange for a Confederate five dollar note. But he did not allow misfortune to overcome him. . . . In order to raise money for immediate needs, he sold the farm and then rented a part of it; but, the purchaser being unable to make payment, the property soon reverted to him. It happened that there was on the farm a small amount of tobacco which the soldiers had not carried away. In a small log cabin this was beaten and sifted, packed in bags and labelled "Pro Bono Publico." It was loaded into a wagon with two barrels of flour and carried to eastern Carolina for sale. The wagon was drawn by two blind mules; to its end was attached a victual box containing a frying pan, two tin plates, a tin cup, a side of bacon, a bushel of meal, and some sweet potatoes. Two blankets, two water buckets, and provender for the horses completed the outfit. At meal time food was prepared, and at night camp was made by the roadside. Such was the first step toward a fortune. The tobacco was easily sold, and with the proceeds bacon was purchased, while the flour was exchanged for two hundred pounds of cotton which was sold in Raleigh. As a present for the children a great luxury was purchased,—a bag of sugar, that being an article which the people could not easily secure.

It was at the end of this journey that Mr. Duke and his younger sons, James Buchanan and Benjamin Newton, decided to continue the home manufacture and the sale of tobacco. A "factory," 20 x 30 feet was built, constructed of logs. This was soon supplanted by an older building, an abandoned residence which had been used as a stable; and it in turn by a new frame structure built for the business. The daily product was 400 or 500 pounds; in 1866 the total amount manufactured was 15,000 pounds, which brought thirty to forty cents per pound after revenue taxes were paid. In 1872 the amount manufactured was 125,000 pounds. . . .

In the meantime "Pro Bono Publico" prospered, and, to facilitate shipping, Washington Duke and his other two sons in 1874 also removed to Durham.

In 1878 all the Dukes in the tobacco business entered into a formal partnership.

W. Duke Sons and Company prospered, but encountered much difficulty in competition with "Bull Durham." With this fact one member of the firm, James Buchanan Duke, was not satisfied. He it was who compared the situation with a stone wall. It was therefore decided, after reports on condition of the trade from Mr. Wright, to manufacture cigarettes as well as smoking tobacco.

Between 1881 and 1884 certain important changes occurred in the cigarette business, and W. Duke Sons and Company very quickly took advantage of them. Of these the most important was machine production. James Bonsack of Virginia invented a machine which was leased to manufacturers for a royalty, and in 1884 two machines were brought to Durham and were installed in the factory of W. Duke Sons and Company. It was very doubtful if the machines would work properly; they had not been a success elsewhere. Moreover, there was supposed to be a prejudice against machine-made cigarettes. For these reasons, the uncertainty regarding the efficiency of the machines and the prejudice against their product, the contract of W. Duke Sons and Company contained a clause by which the company was to have a reduction in the royalty it paid as compared with that required of other companies. Here was an advantage, if only the machines could be made to work satisfactorily. At first there was difficulty, for the machines did not perform effectively. But a correction was soon found. . . .

A second invention was the sliding box, the achievement of James B. Duke himself. Previous to this it was with difficulty that the smoker could carry cigarettes. Sometimes they were put up in small round cartons resembling "tootsie rolls," but these were often crushed, and it was difficult for the smoker to extract a cigarette from the roll. Sometimes, also, they were packed in boxes. The sliding box afforded protection to the cigarette and made it easy of extraction. . . .

About the time the machines were made to work the government tax on cigarettes was reduced from $1.75 to fifty cents per thousand. This, with the cheaper production, made possible a reduction in price; but how much? At that time the smoker paid ten cents for a package of ten cigarettes: but W. Duke Sons and Company, gambling on the savings from economical production and tax reduction, cut the price fifty per cent, and suddenly "Duke of Durham" cigarettes were the cheapest on the market. . . .

The results of all this on the cigarette trade can readily be imagined. With the advantage of reduced price due to machine production and low royalties on the machines, with a manufactured cigarette as good as the hand-made, with safe and convenient packing, Duke cigarettes were an immediate success, and in 1884 the wooden factory was supplanted by the present Liggett and Myers structure. The extent of the increased production is well illustrated by the internal revenue receipts from W. Duke Sons and Company. In 1883 they were $90,000; in 1884, $130,000; in 1885, $138,623; in 1886, $174,217; in 1887, $270,193; in 1888, $517,783; in 1889, $600,000. . . .

Along with the expansion of the business went the famous cigarette war. Never before had the tobacco trade seen such a contest. In the end the rival companies could not compete successfully, and in 1890 four of them joined with W. Duke Sons and Company to form the American Tobacco Company, capitalized at $25,000,000. . . .

DISSOLUTION OF THE TRUST

From this time on until 1911 the "Tobacco Trust" was supreme. This combine came in for its share of vilification during the 90's and there was much prejudice against it. It would seem as if its control of prices paid to the farmer during this period was almost absolute. The actual prices paid to farmers varied from seven to ten cents per pound while the price in terms of purchasing power fluctuated narrowly around ten cents from 1899 to 1911.

In 1911, in the American Tobacco Company case (221 U. S. 108) the Supreme Court of the United States held

STRONG POSITION OF MANUFACTURERS 33

that certain defendants constituted an illegal monopoly and decreed the taking over of the properties of the defendants by fourteen companies. Certain provisions of the decree also involved the partial cessation of the contractual relation between the Imperial and the American Tobacco Companies, especially in the common purchase of leaf tobacco. Certain provisions as to the use of common purchasing agencies, were to be effective for five years, it presumably being the opinion of the court that competition would be restored after that period.

MONOPOLY PRACTICES SINCE DISSOLUTION

However, the operation of the supreme court decree for five years did not permanently change the situation as is indicated by the Federal Trade Commission reports of 1920 and 1922. The 1920 investigation found that the companies had returned to common purchasing agencies.

It would appear, therefore, that eight of the companies subject to the decree during the past two years have either purchased through or from the Universal Co. or its subsidiaries and three through the International Planters Corporation.

The report points out that the formation of the Universal Leaf Tobacco Company was a major event in the structure of the tobacco market. It was a holding company controlling the stocks of twenty-four subsidiary purchasing companies and buying in its own name. Some of its principal stockholders and officials were former officials of the big four. This company purchased the same grades of tobacco for several of the manufacturers. The language of the report is as follows:[3]

[3] Report of the Federal Trade Commission on the Tobacco Industry, December, 1920, pp. 157-158, 162.

It is submitted, that if these transactions occurred prior to November, 1916, they would have been considered as violations of the decree. In considering this question, it should be remembered that at the time the decree was entered, there was no organization in existence similar to the two named. Particular attention is called to the fact that both of the common agents mentioned were formed just about the time the limitation as to this practice expired. Also that several of the officials of the Universal Co. were formerly connected with some of the larger interests. . . .

Although the language of the degree "doing business directly or indirectly under any other than its own corporate name" is broad, it was apparently aimed at companies owned by the defendants in which their ownership was not disclosed, and who were engaged in selling the manufactured product. It is believed, however, that this provision should be modified so as to include the purchase of leaf tobacco through agencies not disclosed to the trade because the public in selling leaf tobacco is entitled to know with whom it is dealing, as well as when it is purchasing the manufactured product.

It was shown in the preceding section that the Universal Leaf Tobacco Co. purchased for and sold to the Imperial Tobacco Co. out of the 1918 crop and during the same period purchased for and sold to the Export Leaf Tobacco Co., a considerable quantity of tobacco. In 1919, the same company purchased various types of tobacco on order for the Imperial Co., and also for both the Export Leaf Tobacco Co. and the Black Horse Tobacco. Sales were also made to these companies from their own purchases during this year. This would apparently violate this part of the provision of the decree prohibiting the two companies from employing a common agent. It was further shown that in 1918 six of the disintegrated companies either purchased through or from the Universal Co. various kinds of tobacco, and in 1919 that four of the disintegrated companies purchased through or from the same agency that was used by the two British companies. This fact would indicate that the last clause of the provision which prohibits them from uniting with the other companies named in the decree in the employment of a common agency had also been violated. . . .

It is recommended that the decree above referred to be modified as follows:

1. That the provision relating to the use of common agencies by the defendant companies, in the purchase of leaf tobacco, which expired by limitation November, 1916, be revived and made permanent.

STRONG POSITION OF MANUFACTURERS

2. That the provision relating to the defendant companies doing business under any other than their own corporate name or that of a subsidiary corporation controlled by them be made specific so as to include the purchase of leaf tobacco through agencies not disclosed to the trade.

The Commission also recommends that a Federal system of grading leaf tobacco be established by the Department of Agriculture. The authority to establish such a system apparently has been given that department under section 19 of the United States warehouse act. It is believed that this would tend to stabilize market values under abnormal conditions such as prevailed during part of last season.

The 1922 report found as follows:[4]

1. That beginning with the spring of 1921 there was a nation-wide movement having for its object the organization of jobbers' associations to fix prices by eliminating price cutting among jobbers. This movement was fostered and aided principally by the American Tobacco Co., P. Lorillard Co., and Liggett & Myers Tobacco Co., followed by the Tobacco Products Corporation, Bloch Bros. Tobacco Co., and Scotten-Dillon Co.

Certain of these manufacturers, in combination with the jobbers, refused to sell to those jobbers who cut below the prices established by the jobbers' associations. This refusal grew out of the fact that previous to the spring of 1921 competition was resulting in a material lowering of the prices which jobbers charged to retailers, and, in turn, are the prices which retailers charged to consumers, which apparently caused the manufacturers to fear that these price reductions would mean that the manufacturers would be compelled ultimately to reduce their own prices.

Combinations of jobbers against price cutters were greatly encouraged by certain circulars sent to the trade by some of the manufacturers named, in which each company made clear that jobbers were expected not to sell at cut prices and that if they did they would be cut off from the company's list of customers. There were meetings held at which the members of associations were encouraged by representatives of one or another of the manufacturers to keep prices up and were assured that the price-cutting jobbers were being stricken from the list of customers to whom the manufacturer would sell. In effecting many local or sectional combinations of jobbers personal visits were made to the individual jobbers by agents or

[4] Report of the Federal Trade Commission: *Prices of Tobacco Products*, 1922, pp. 7, 8, 9.

officials of the manufacturers fostering this movement and by representatives of jobbers' associations already formed in other communities, who undertook to convince, and who at times even instructed, members of the trade that they should not sell below list prices less the agreed discount.

A few cases were found where the jobbers went so far as to enter into a signed agreement with each other to maintain prices. Such an agreement was made by Rhode Island jobbers, together with certain Massachusetts jobbers. The commission has in its possession the original of this agreement signed by 18 jobbers.

Committees from some of the jobbers' associations went to New York City and conferred with officials of certain of the above-named manufacturers to find out their policy in regard to coöperation with associations in price maintenance and reported that these officials assured them of encouragement and support by their respective companies. Letters in the possession of the commission show cases of jobbers being actually refused supplies by some of these manufacturers in order to compel them to cease price cutting.

In asserting the legality of this cutting off of price disturbers George W. Hill, vice president of the American Tobacco Co., writing on August 5, 1931, to a jobber, said:

"It is not our purpose here to establish the price at which our merchandise is sold; that is a matter which rests entirely in the hands of our customers in any given community.

"We have no hesitation, however, in assuring you that where a customary price prevails in a given community we are entirely within our legal rights in removing from our direct list of customers any customer who by selling our merchandise at less than the prevailing price in that community thereby destroys the interest of our company."

On the other hand, L. B. McKitterick, president of M. Melachrino & Co., a subsidiary of the Tobacco Products Corporation, writing to a representative at San Francisco on October 14. viewed the practice as illegal, saying:

"You can explain to their jobbers the law as it stands to-day, which is that if a manufacturer joins with a jobbers' association in compelling an individual jobber to unite with the jobbers' association or agree to give the same discounts, a conspiracy in restraint of the trade results, which is absolutely in violation of the law, and not only will the manufacturer be guilty of conspiracy, but also the jobbers' association."

The inquiry as to association activities incidentally developed the fact that during recent years one large tobacco manufacturer, the American Tobacco Co., has given to favored jobber customers secret bonuses or rebates in round amounts, ranging from a few hundred dollars to several thousands of dollars at a time. These payments have usually been made semiannually, and recipients have regarded them as secret and confidential. In speaking of these payments, one of the jobbers stated that he regarded them as secret rebates; that he looked upon them as "tips," and as "so much fodder hung on the end of a stick and tied to a mule's head in such a way that he could nibble at it without getting it all, to urge him on." . . .

3. While no conclusive evidence was found of collusion to depress the prices paid to the growers for the 1920 leaf, it appears that a few large buyers had a dominant position and each purchased only a certain percentage of the offerings; that common buying agencies were used, and that secret purchases were made through independent dealers while the ultimate purchasers held off the market, or practically so. This situation was fully described in a report by this commission to the House of Representatives on December 11, 1920, which recommended that the temporary injunction against the successor companies prohibiting their use of common purchasing agencies for leaf tobacco be revived and made permanent, and that they be also prohibited from purchasing except under their own names. That report and recommendation was duly submitted to the Attorney General. This recommendation is urgently renewed. . . .

The 1925 report did not investigate the retail market practices but reaffirmed the 1920 report as to practices in buying leaf from farmers. Thus we have evidence of continuing monopoly action both in buying the raw material and selling the finished product. In spite of the recommendations of the Federal Trade Commission nothing seems to have been done about the situation.

It may be said that, while the 1911 decree theoretically dissolved the tobacco trust, the result, as far as the domestic manufacture of cigarettes was concerned, was that there were only four units and these were powerful concerns. None of them operate anywhere near the margin in production costs. In spite of all federal laws and investigations these have persisted as a quasi-monopoly of the cigarette trade and have gone at least to the limit of the law in their agreements.

There seems, however, to be one rift in the lute—the Reynolds Company—which has grown to be the largest of the four in income. This company, in the 1920 investigation, seemed to go along with the others in buying policies but the 1922 investigation of actually illegal practices had the following to say:[5]

There was one important successor company, namely, R. J. Reynolds Tobacco Co., which refused to lend any support to these conspiracies, but actively opposed them. In spite of strong pressure exerted by jobbers and jobbers' associations, the Reynolds Co. stood stanchly against the practices of certain of its competitors designed to induce or force jobbers to enter and maintain price agreements, and in this respect is deserving of commendation. . . .

In dealing with the coöperative, the Reynolds Company also seemed to adopt a different attitude toward the farmers' efforts, for they purchased tobacco freely from the association while the others practically boycotted it in its last years of operation.

Confirmation of this monopolistic condition is found in succeeding chapters on the reaction of retail price to taxes which is just what would be expected in monopoly selling, and the reaction of farm price to supply which is just what would be expected of monopoly buying.

There are other considerations which contribute to the well entrenched position of the companies:

(1) They are engaged in an industry subject to the law of diminishing costs. The increase in volume of cigarette

[5] Report of the Federal Trade Commission on Prices of Tobacco Products, 1922, p. 6.

STRONG POSITION OF MANUFACTURERS 39

production has been tremendous, but reference to Table X (Chapter V) will show that a large proportion of their costs is in selling, advertising, expenditures, and in fixed overhead costs which diminish per unit as production increases. Leaf and labor costs, which tend to decrease in cost per unit slightly with production increases, form only thirty-six per cent of the total costs.

(2) Another consideration is the nature of the demand which, as will appear in a later chapter, keeps increasing at a rapid rate, regardless of minor fluctuations in retail price.

(3) The tremendous carry-over or stock on hand also puts them in an independent market position.

TABLE V
RATE OF RETURN OF NET INCOME TO INVESTMENT

	American Tobacco Co.	Liggett & Myers Tobacco Co.	P. Lorillard Co.	R. J. Reynolds Tobacco Co.	Average
1916:	Per cent	Per cent	Per cent	Per cent	Per cent
As reported...	9.4	10.6	11.1	30.4	12.0
As revised....	12.3	15.2	14.0	32.0	16.1
1917:					
As reported...	10.1	10.8	13.2	28.3	13.0
As revised....	12.7	14.8	21.9	29.2	18.0
1918:					
As reported...	11.2	9.9	11.1	13.8	11.2
As revised....	20.9	19.8	18.4	26.1	21.2
1919:					
As reported...	10.6	7.9	9.7	16.7	10.7
As revised....	14.0	10.2	7.5	19.5	13.0
1920:					
As reported...	9.5	8.8	11.3	13.2	10.3
As revised....	11.8	11.5	11.8	15.0	12.5
Average 5 years:					
As reported...	10.2	9.4	11.2	17.9	11.3
As revised....	14.5	14.0	14.0	21.8	15.8

EARNINGS

The strong position of these companies is further emphasized by their annual financial reports. In 1922 the Federal Trade Commission revised the reports of the companies to eliminate some of their good will and adjust their reported profits. See Table V.[6]

The following figures from the 1929 *Annual Review of the Tobacco Industry* (Chas. D. Barney & Co.) indicate that this high rate of earning has continued except for the smallest company, Lorillard, which has been encountering difficulties in marketing a new cigarette.

TABLE VI
EARNING AND INVESTMENT OF TOBACCO COMPANIES 1928

Company	Investment (excluding good will)	Net earnings available for dividends	Percentage return on investment
R. J. Reynolds	$156,260,000	$30,172,600	19.3
American Tobacco	177,100,000	25,014,400	14.1
Liggett & Myers	149,800,000	19,408,600	13.0
P. Lorillard	81,400,000	1,817,400	2.2

Thus, to deal with the hundreds of thousands of poorly organized, poorly informed farmers, there are four highly organized and powerful domestic tobacco companies with a tremendous surplus supply of the commodity on hand and with profits piling up because of monopoly advantages, diminishing costs, and a demand which shows a tendency to keep climbing regardless of minor price fluctuations. Under those circumstances the "big four" have piled up enormous profits and have been able to exert great influence not only

[6] Report of the Federal Trade Commission on Prices of Tobacco Products, 1922, p. 35.

on the retail price of their product but also on the farm price of leaf tobacco.

The following is a complete statement of earnings from the same source:

TABLE VII
NET EARNINGS AVAILABLE FOR DIVIDENDS IN MILLIONS

Year	R. J. Reynolds Tobacco Co.	American Tobacco Co.	Liggett & Myers Tobacco Co.	P. Lorillard Co.	Combined Total
1914	3	12	5	3	23
1915	5	11	7	4	26
1916	8	12	7	5	32
1917	10	13	7	6	37
1918	7	17	8	6	37
1919	11	16	6	5	38
1920	11	15	8	7	40
1921	16	18	10	6	51
1922	20	19	10	7	56
1923	23	18	10	5	55
1924	24	21	12	5	62
1925	25	22	15	6	68
1926	26	22	18	4	71
1927	29	23	19	2	74
1928	30	25	19	2	76

In the light of the recent enthusiasm for mergers this is an aspect of monopoly which needs re-examination. The discussions of trusts in the '90's had much to say of their effects on the price of their finished product but little to say regarding their effect on the prices which they paid for the raw materials. The remainder of this volume is an exposition of the action of raw tobacco price in which the highly organized position of the tobacco companies is a dominant factor.

CHAPTER IV

THE AUCTION MARKET SYSTEM

TO THE uninitiated a visit to the auction market is confusing. The piles of tobacco are in long rows stretching across the warehouse floor. Men are grouped around one of the piles. The auctioneer mumbles a queer jargon, but presently words begin to emerge "Sweet as honey, honey, honey, gimme thirty gimme thirty." A man winks "thirty, thirty. Any more?" Another nods, "thirty and a quarter." An entry is made on the tag and the crowd moves to the next pile where the same performance is staged with lightning rapidity. The auctioneer chants and sways. The buyers nod, wink, and gesticulate. The farmers look on hopefully rather enjoying the annual show.

It is easy to distinguish the farmers from the buyers. The former are in "town" clothes and look uncertain. The latter are well dressed and assured.

PROCEDURE

It is thus that the farmer and the manufacturer's representative meet and through this medium that a three hundred million dollar crop changes hands.

The farmer brings his tobacco and it is weighed, tagged, and placed on the floor for sale in baskets. Each pile is auctioned separately and the high bid and name of the bidder entered on the tag. The farmer has the right to reject the bid but there are many reasons why he seldom does. In the first place he pays an auction fee each time. Again he does not wish to hang around town and pay lodging while looking for a higher bid and he does not wish to haul his tobacco home and run the risk of its deterioration while he waits a better price. He is in a buyer's market.

Then, as we have previously stated, most of the farmers do not really know what grade of tobacco they have raised and what the demand for it is. They have no way of judging whether the price bid is fair or not, except by talking around with others who have sold tobacco that day. The government system of grading will go a long way toward correcting this lack of knowledge.

Nor are the buyers any too sure of the *exact* nature of the pile of tobacco. These sales are conducted at the rate of 300 per hour, sometimes faster. Lightning appraisal must be made in order to auction from two to five of these lots to the minute.

Buyers, however, have this advantage. They are buying certain grades within certain limits and they can average their purchases so that their total purchase will be within the limits, but some lots may fall short and others greatly exceed the average. Thus some farmers gain what others lose in this averaging process. This is known as the "take from some and give to others" system. It renders the auction prices very erratic. The farmer has no assurance whatever that good quality will bring its proper premium, or that poor quality will not be unduly penalized.

VARIATIONS IN PRICE

Playful farmers have sometimes moved the same basket of tobacco about on the floor so that it would be bid on several times by the same buyers the same day with the startling results that the high bids often varied over 100 per cent. Sapiro describes one of these incidents as follows:[1] "Some

[1] Aaron Sapiro, "Rolling Their Own," *Survey*, April 1, 1923.

44   THE PLIGHT OF CIGARETTE TOBACCO

growers agreed to sell their tobacco in the first row, then changed the tags and move it to the second and third rows. One farmer sold the same basket of tobacco ten times, with prices ranging from 8 to 28 cents per pound. The same buyer who bought it for 28 cents had also bought it for 11 cents."[2]

Under the government grading system the tag showing the weight of the tobacco is stamped with the grade also and finally with the high bids. Compilation of some of these bids on the same grade of tobacco, the same day, in the same market show that wild fluctuations in price of much over 100 per cent are the rule rather than the exception.[3]

This system works no serious hardship on the trained buyer, for as we have explained, he is averaging his purchases. While he may be forced a little high on one lot he can make it up on others. The farmer, on the other hand, is as likely as not to be one of those who suffers by this averaging process.

[2] Nor is this phenomenon of erratic prices confined to tobacco. The United States Department of Agriculture in its several studies of cotton prices, under market conditions more subject to the play of free competition than the auction system of tobacco, discovered price ranges in bales of the same grade on the same day as follows:

Variations in Prices Paid Middling Cotton in Certain Oklahoma Towns*

Place	Price Bale No. 1 reduced to 500 pounds	Price Bale No. 2 reduced to 500 pounds	Range in Price
Ryan	$51.25	$54.58	$3.33
Norman	55.00	57.50	2.50
Terrell	55.80	59.50	3.70
Mt. Park	56.25	59.00	2.75
Caddo	55.00	59.38	4.38
Eric	52.00	58.00	6.00

* Robert H. Montgomery, *The Cooperative Pattern in Cotton*, p. 14, (MacMillan, 1929).

The table gives ten other instances with similar ranges.

However, it would seem that the auction prices of tobacco fluctuate more widely than the prices of raw cotton.

[3] Tests made by Mr. Clifton J. Bradley on price of tobacco by grade.

In fact it is a frequent practice for buyers to shade up the price for a lot when they know that it belongs to a large and influential farmer. Other poor unknowns must make up for that. It is for this reason that tenants much prefer that their landlord sell their tobacco for them rather than to put it on the floor in their own names.

COLLUSION IN BUYING AND HOLDING OFF THE MARKET

By the auction system most of the tobacco passed from the farmer to the manufacturer, through the buyer, who is the direct representative of the manufacturer, and who transports the purchase direct to the depository of the manufacturer. There are few speculators in tobacco. These known as "pin hookers" usually operate on a small scale. Aside from the large manufacturers, there are a few large dealers who buy little tobacco for speculative purposes but who often act as the buying agents for manufacturers and who do this buying under instruction just as the regularly employed buyers do.

The leaf dealers make possible the practice of buying under cover as a dealer may be buying the same grade for several companies. Of this practice, frowned upon by the Federal Trade Commission, the investigation of that body in 1920 had the following to say:[4]

According to the testimony of numerous tobacco producers, dealers, warehousemen, and buyers, as well as the correspondence of the large manufacturers and dealers, one of the most important causes of the decline in prices of leaf tobacco during the 1919-20 season was "holding off" the market and "buying under cover," indulged in by the large tobacco manufacturers. The effect of these practices varied, but was most apparent in those markets where the companies

[4] Report of the Federal Trade Commission on the Tobacco Industry, December, 1920, pp. 50, 53.

using the methods were important purchasers. As a general proposition, it is recognized by those experienced in the trade, that "holding off" the market, even temporarily, by any concern which purchases a substantial percentage of the tobacco sold on that market will have a direct effect on the prices being paid. Also it is recognized that where a large tobacco purchaser buys its requirements "under cover" through a dealer already on the market, competition is lessened and the price is affected.

The extent of such methods and the effect thereof varied in the different localities, being apparent in the burley, dark western, and bright southern districts in the order given.

* * * * * *

Another factor which has a direct effect on prices is the fact that in some cases a dealer will purchase tobacco for several companies. It has a tendency to lower prices in that competition is eliminated in proportion to the number of companies involved, providing competitive tobaccos are being purchased in this manner. The fact that the less important users of tobacco purchased through the same agency, would, of course, not affect the market appreciably and would operate to their advantage in that the expenses of separate buying organizations would be saved. However, the practice is not limited to the smaller companies, and in recent years some of the large companies have used the same agencies, although maintaining extensive buying organizations of their own.

Since this investigation two other Federal Trade Commission investigations, in 1922 and 1925, have been made without revealing any substantial change in these methods. In fact both of these later reports refer to the 1920 report as representative of the conditions.

Another practice often attributed to the manufacturers in their buying policies is collusion in setting the limits for their buyers.[5]

While opinions differ as to the existence of competition among the buyers of leaf tobacco, and no conclusive evidence of collusion to bring about the decline is at hand, attention should be called to the

[5] Report of the Federal Trade Commission on the Tobacco Industry, December, 1920, pp. 51, 144.

THE AUCTION MARKET SYSTEM 47

fact that in each of the chief growing areas the buying is centered in very few hands.

Our 1919 crop of manufacturing and export tobaccos, as shown by the estimates given in Chapter I, was 1,158,000,000 pounds and constituted about 85 per cent of the total crop. The purchases of these types during the season by two closely affiliated British manufacturers, the Italian and French régies, and two dealers largely engaged in exporting tobacco amounted to more than 354,000,000 pounds, and were thus equivalent to over 30 per cent of the crop. The four tobacco manufacturers (R. J. Reynolds Tobacco Co., Liggett & Myers Tobacco Co., the American Tobacco Co., and P. Lorillard Co.), sometimes called the "Big Four," and the three snuff companies (American Snuff Co., Weyman-Bruton Co., and George W. Helme Co.), that succeeded to the domestic manufacturing business of the combination under the decree of dissolution in 1911, purchased over 395,000,000 pounds, or an amount equivalent to more than 60 per cent of the remainder of the crop, the four tobacco manufacturers taking about seven times as much as the snuff companies. The purchases of one of the British manufacturers alone was equivalent to 15.4 per cent of the 1919 crop, and of the two combined to 23.5 per cent, and those of one of the "successor" companies alone was equivalent to 23.9 per cent of the remainder of the crop.

Particular attention was paid to the charge that there was collusion among the buyers of leaf tobacco, especially the large interests—that is, whether there was any agreement or understanding between these companies to manipulate the market. It was believed that if such agreements existed the buyers' procedure in buying would render it evident to experienced persons on the floor while such buying was going on, although the buyers themselves might not be aware of such fact. The warehousemen and independent dealers, therefore, who accompanied the sales were particularly questioned as to evidence of the action of the buyers on the floor.

It is only fair to state that many of the independent dealers and warehousemen in their interviews were unequivocal in their statements that they did not observe anything in their operations on the market that would indicate that there was collusion on the part of manufacturers and large dealers in buying of leaf tobacco. However, there were many who expressed a contrary opinion.

The independent dealers stating that there was collusion apparently based their opinions on the following:

48 THE PLIGHT OF CIGARETTE TOBACCO

That common buyers were employed.

That many of the companies confined their purchases to a certain percentage of the offerings, not bidding above a certain price.

That there apparently was a disposition not to bid against each other on some grades; and that they bid actively against each other on some markets and do not compete at all on other markets.

However, it would seem that so crude a practice as collusion is unnecessary. Buyers are not on a market for more than two or three days before they know very well the limits within which their fellow buyers are operating. Constant communication informs their superiors of the situation and they are ordered to adjust their bids to those of the other buyers, or to "stand pat," or to cease bidding on certain grades provided the manufacturer sees that he has no pressing need for these grades or thinks that they will later come into the market in sufficient quantity to satisfy his requirements at prices lower than the current bids.

Thus it becomes a game among the buyers,—not to bid on the merits of each lot of tobacco, but to secure their requirements at as low a price as possible, figuring always on the supply coming into the market rather than the demand. For the demand, as we shall explain more fully later, is cushioned by the tremendous supplies of leaf tobacco kept in storage over several years by the manufacturers. Under these circumstances actual collusion in fixing bidding limits is hardly necessary—a gentleman's agreement not to "hog the market" would seem to be ample enough.

AUCTION MARKETING VS. COÖPERATIVE MARKETING

This machinery of marketing may be contrasted with the system which the Tri-State Tobacco Grower's Association endeavored unsuccessfully to set up. Under the coöperative

THE AUCTION MARKET SYSTEM 49

plan the farmers were to pool their tobacco in coöperative warehouses, have it scientifically graded by experts and sold through coöperative salesmen to the buyers of the tobacco companies. The association bought an expensive chain of warehouses, worked out a logical system of grades, and employed an expert corps of graders. However the coöperative was not strong enough to take over the *whole* warehouse machinery; hence, for the period of its existence, auction warehouses and coöperative warehouses were operated side by side, and coöperative marketing was competing with auction marketing.

It soon became apparent that the two could not coexist and that the one having the buyers favor would win out. The auction warehouses had this favor. It was manifested by the hand-to-mouth purchases from the coöp by all but one of the tobacco companies and by the shading of prices in favor of non-members who sold their tobacco in the auction market. This higher price to the non-member made members disgruntled and led to contract breaking.

Overtly the tobacco companies made no move against the coöperative but the tobacco trade journal became violently anti-coöperative and floods of anti-coöperative advertising appeared. Some of these issues were subsidized by the tobacco companies.

The Tobacco Farmer, a journal financed almost entirely by tobacco company advertisements and warehousemen's subscriptions, appeared in 1923. The editor wrote as follows to an official of the Imperial Tobacco Company in soliciting an advertisement:[6]

---
[6] Federal Trade Commission, *The American Tobacco Company and the Imperial Tobacco Company,* 1920, p. 66.

"My DEAR MR. CARLTON: I am writing you hurriedly and confidentially. As you know, Mr. Carlton, I am making a strong fight against the proposed coöperative marketing proposition. I am greatly encouraged over my efforts. I am told that if I had started out two months earlier I could have sidetracked the whole business. ..."

In May another special issue was gotten out which the editor said would give the association a "solar plexus blow." In explaining his plans for this edition the editor wrote:[7]

It is my purpose now Mr. Reed to get out for leading markets an edition of my journal which will contain arguments, etc. against [sic] coöperative marketing plan. The edition will be a strong one and will cover all points. I cannot hope to make any money out of the proposition, as I am going to sell to each one of the markets as many of these copies as possible for 12 cents per copy. We will go to the sheriff's office in each county and secure names of tobacco farmers and at our expense mail to them a copy of the special edition.

I am arranging to get out as soon as possible a huge special edition of my journal to cover the States of North Carolina, South Carolina and Virginia. If possible I want to send out 50,000 or more of this special edition. These papers will be sold to warehousemen and dealers at cost, and mailed, from lists furnished by each market, direct to farmers.

It has also been alleged that, during the time when the coöperative and auction systems existed side by side, farmers who "split" their sales, sending part to the coöperative and part to the auction floor, and let this be known, were given a higher price by the buyers for the portion placed on the auction floor. The investigation of the Federal Trade Commission of 1925 did not uncover any conclusive evidence on this point, as the practice was flatly denied by all buyers. Numbers of farmers, however, were equally positive that the part of their "split" crop sold on the auction floor brought a higher price than the part sent to the coöperative.

[7] *Ibid.*, pp. 67, 68.

Subsequent studies of tobacco prices during the operation of the association have revealed an *average* auction floor price higher than the coöperative price. However, since no information is available as to the relative grades, this evidence is not conclusive.

It is worthwhile to inquire just why the tobacco companies should have opposed the coöperative. On the face of it there were certain advantages to them as well as to the farmers in such an organization. They were able to buy intelligently graded tobacco instead of making hit and miss purchases by the averaging program. They could buy in bulk and not in small lots. By doing this they could in time doubtless have reduced their buying force.

But there was the human equation. Under the militant fire-eating stimulus of its organizers, the association started avowedly to do battle with the tobacco companies and the auction warehouse system, and it was only human for the companies and warehousemen to meet them in a similar spirit of antagonism. In one of his early speeches at Wilson, N. C., a large tobacco center, Sapiro told the auction warehousemen that if coöperative marketing succeeded grass would grow in the streets of Wilson. And it is conceivable that none of the Wilson tobacco dealers desired this to happen.

More fundamental, however, was the fact that the former Tri-State Association seemed to be aiming at monopoly of supply and emphasized in their campaigns the possibility of price control. This, the manufacturers naturally opposed. The tobacco associations now in process of organization seem to be avoiding this obstacle by aiming at a more limited pool, and by placing emphasis on such services as grading, information, and market economy, rather than on price dictation.

This less antagonistic program will probably merit less opposition from the manufacturers.

On the other hand the present auction market system has one manifest advantage for the farmer which the coöp could not provide, that is the auction market absorbs all the tobacco which comes in sight and tenders the farmer spot cash. To handle the flue-cured crop alone for cash at 20 cents per pound the coöperative organization would need from $125,-000,000 to $150,000,000 annually, and no such sum was available to the association. The coöperative marketers, therefore, received a part cash payment and a "participation certificate" while their non-coöperative neighbors received cash down.

GOVERNMENT GRADING

A distinct advance over the old blind auction but by no means a substitute for coöperative marketing is the system of auction of government graded tobacco which is now beginning to spread. As early as 1920 the Federal Trade Commission noted that the lack of grades worked a hardship on both buyer and seller.[8]

Mention might also be made here that the lack of a uniform system of grading is harmful in many ways. Dealers complain that unscrupulous growers increase the weight of their product by adding moisture and foreign substances, and also by attempting to deceive the purchaser as to the quality of their offerings. The latter practice is usually termed nesting. It might also be stated that where tobacco is sold in hogsheads the packer does not always put tobacco of uniform quality in the container. On the hogshead markets three samples are taken from the container—i.e., one from near the top, another from near the middle, and the other from the bottom. On the other hand, the grower contends that he has no assurance that his crop of certain grade brings its value as compared with the same grade of another grower. This is due to the fact that each buyer

[8] Report of the Federal Trade Commission on Tobacco Industry, December, 1920, pp. 37, 38.

following his own ideas as to grades, uses markings which convey no meaning to the seller. Many of those interviewed stated that they knew of cases where the crops of certain growers would be run up to above their real value. In a few cases, it was stated that one could employ a buyer or warehouseman to run up his tobacco if he was willing to pay for it, the usual charge for such service being $1 per hundred pounds.

All in all, it would seem that the difficulties presented might be corrected by the enactment of a Federal law providing for a uniform system of grading leaf tobacco. The Bureau of Markets of the United States Department of Agriculture now has under consideration a plan looking to some system of uniform grading and classification in connection with the Federal warehouse act. (39 U. S. State., 466, as amended by 41 U. S. Stat., 234, 266.) Hearings during the month of October, 1920, were held at various points, but the department's conclusions have not as yet been made public.

Yet when the coöperative association worked out a system of grading designed to cover all types of tobacco, the companies alleged that the lack of correspondence between these grades and their own was the chief reason why they did not purchase from the association.

Mr. F. B. Wilkinson, who worked out this system of grades for the Tri-State Association, has been retained by the Department of Agriculture to adapt the system to all types of tobacco, and the government now grades the farmer's tobacco for a small fee provided the farmer wishes it.

In the flue-cured area this grading service was offered on three markets in 1929, Lake City, S. C., Smithfield, N. C., and South Hill, Va. At Lake City about 20 per cent of the tobacco was graded in 1929 and at Smithfield about 25 per cent, while at South Hill 19 per cent was graded. This is an insignificant proportion of the flue-cured crop.[9] Arrangements are, however, being made to extend this grading service as rapidly as possible.

[9] The service was extended to a number of other markets in 1930.

This system makes available for the first time certain knowledge about the marketing of tobacco which should prove of increasing value to the trade. For the first time, in 1929, the companies were required to report stocks on hand by grades. Formerly they reported merely by type. This innovation will give valuable information about the stock on hand of each grade and the disappearance of that grade between reports.

As a larger proportion of the tobacco is graded it will show the proportions of each grade in the various markets. This grading, with the prices obtained, lays the foundation for needed farm economic research in the profits of tobacco culture and the effects of various methods of culture on quality. Finally, the system, for the first time, furnishes prices by grade, rather than general average prices which, taken apart from grade, are not so significant in shedding light upon the price situation.

Summary

The auction market system whereby the farmer and the manufacturer's buyer meet is characterized by the rapidity of the sales and the wide fluctuation in price. While the buyers have a good general idea of what they are buying, the sellers, if their tobacco is ungraded, do not know the exact quality of what they are selling. The buyers are further protected in that they are buying large quantities within limits or at averages which permit them to make up for over-bids by compensating under-bids. The auction market practices of the companies have in the past frequently been shown to be monopolistic in that companies sometimes hold off the market altogether and sometimes buy through dealers, "under cover." Also there are so few buyers that

THE AUCTION MARKET SYSTEM 55

the buyers of each company can keep up very closely with the practices of the others and regulate their policy accordingly. During the period of existence of the coöperative, auction marketing and coöperative marketing were competing with the result that coöperation lost out. The new system of government grading of tobacco for the auction market is between the two and offers manifest advantages in informing the farmer as to what he is selling and safe-guarding the buyer from snap judgments. It also forms the basis of valuable information on tobacco, more exact than has hitherto been available.

CHAPTER V

THE FEDERAL CIGARETTE TAX

IN THE early days of the republic, the States, very jealous of their taxing powers, left the Federal government little to tax besides tobacco, liquor, and imports. Internal revenues from tobacco, therefore, for a long time, played an important part in the support of the government.

AMOUNT

Tobacco taxes still form about twelve per cent of the United States' revenues, even though income, inheritance, and other taxes have been added. The tobacco tax now amounts to over four hundred million dollars, of which cigarettes bear almost three-fourths. Table VIII gives the collections of internal revenue from all tobacco, exclusive of tax on cigarette papers and tubes, and from cigarettes alone, from 1910 to 1928. In 1910 the tax on cigarettes was only eight out of a total of fifty-eight millions but in 1928 it was about three hundred out of four hundred millions. With reference to the total farm value of the flue-cured crop, which is about three hundred millions, it is evident that the government gets as much by taxing the half of the crop which is consumed at home as the farmer receives for the whole crop.

Table VIII also reduces these figures to a per capita basis. The per capita burden of the tobacco tax has also increased rapidly from seventy-four cents per person in 1912 to over three dollars in 1926. The per capita cigarette tax accounted for about two and a quarter dollars of this three dollars and a quarter.

THE FEDERAL CIGARETTE TAX

TABLE VIII
INTERNAL REVENUE FROM TOBACCO AND CIGARETTES

Fiscal Year	Total (*)		Per capita (†)	
	From all tobacco (millions)	From all cigarettes (millions)	From all tobacco	From all cigarettes
1928	395	301	....	....
1927	375	279	....	....
1926	370	255	3.16	2.18
1925	344	225	3.04	1.98
1924	325	204	2.91	1.82
1923	308	183	2.79	1.65
1922	270	150	2.48	1.37
1921	254	135	2.37	1.26
1920	294	151	2.78	1.42
1919	205	91	1.93	.85
1918	156	66	1.48	.63
1917	103	38	1.00	.37
1916	88	26	.86	.26
1915	80	21	.80	.21
1914	80	21	.81	.21
1913	76	18	.79	.18
1912	70	14	.74	.15
1911	67	12	.72	.14
1910	58	8	.65	.09

* Stocks of Leaf Tobacco—U. S. Bureau of the Census, 1928.
† Report of Commissioner Internal Revenue, 1922, p. 122. 1928, p. 113.Per Capita based on intercensal estimates of population.

Cigarettes are also subject to a variety of local taxes. Many states have stamp taxes and many municipalities impose licenses upon dealers in cigarettes. It is, however, with the federal tax that this discussion is primarily concerned. These taxes are levied on the general theory that they are luxury taxes and are borne by the retail purchaser of the product. The evidence seems to indicate, however, that the case is not so simple.

CHANGES IN RATE

The Federal cigarette tax is a stamp tax levied on the basis of one thousand cigarettes sold in the United States.

It is larger on cigarettes which weigh more than three pounds per thousand than on cigarettes which weigh less than three pounds per thousand. The actual amount paid per pound of manufactured tobacco, therefore, fluctuates with the number of pounds put into a thousand cigarettes and with the number withdrawn tax free for export.

The following table gives the rate per thousand, on cigarettes weighing not more than three pounds per one thousand, levied by recent internal revenue acts:

STAMP TAX EFFECTIVE

	Per 1,000	Per package of 20
Aug. 5, 1909	$1.25	.025
Oct. 4, 1917	1.65	.033
Nov. 2, 1917	2.05	.041
Feb. 26, 1919	3.00	.060

INCIDENCE AND RELATION TO FARM PRICE

When the cigarette tax was increased for war revenues the retail price was also increased. The increase on the standard low price brands was from 15 cents retail to 20 cents retail per package, or from $7.50 to $10.00 per thousand cigarettes (Table IX, Diagram III). This was a $2.50 increase in retail price as against about $2.00 increase in internal revenue per thousand cigarettes. When these prices are expressed as a ratio to the cost of living, however, it is apparent that the price of cigarettes fell. The deflated decrease was from $6.59 per thousand in 1916 to $5.38 per thousand in 1919. Thus there was a decrease in price per thousand with an increase in the deflated tax. Seemingly none of the tax increase was shifted to the consumer.

After the war, however, notwithstanding the fact that taxes remained unchanged in rate, the deflated tax increased still further, but the pre-war retail price was restored, slightly reducing the deflated price. Other items of cost had also been greatly reduced from war levels but not cut to pre-war levels. The outstanding factor was the tremendous increase in the volume of production. Thus with each change from 1916 to 1922 there was an increase in real tax but a decrease in real retail price. Seemingly the manufacturers did not pass along to the consumer any of this deflated tax increase. Farm prices during this period fluctuated. With an increased tax in 1919 farm prices had also increased. With the further increase in real tax in 1922, real prices paid the farmer for leaf tobacco declined. See Diagram III.

TABLE IX
TAX, RETAIL PRICE AND FARM PRICE OF CIGARETTE TOBACCO

Year	Price per thousand cigarettes	Deflated price and tax per thousand cigarettes (Deflated with retail index)		Deflated with retail index less agricultural commodities
		Price	Tax	North Carolina farm price per pound
1922	$ 7.50	$5.28	$2.110	19.9
1919	10.00	5.38	1.613	26.1
1916	7.50	6.59	1.106	16.3

When the retail price was 20 cents in 1920 the Federal Trade Commission worked out the distribution of cost of two brands of cigarettes. See Table X.

The difference in cost and invoice price, in so far as it is not accounted for by profits, represents jobbers' and dealers' discounts. The leaf cost includes the price paid to the farmer, plus redrying and processing, and interest on money invested in stored stocks.

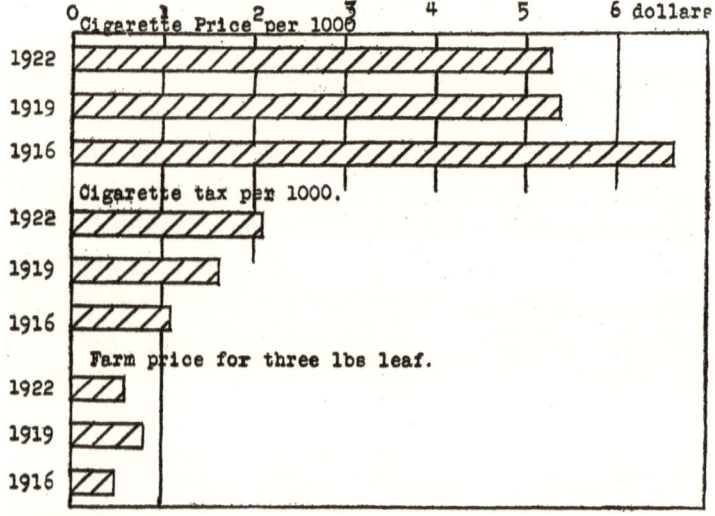

DIAGRAM III
Relation of Retail Price, Tax and Farm Price (Deflated)

It will be noted from this table, first, that the tax of $3.00 per thousand prevailing at this time constituted nearly half of the total costs. Second, that with this tax and with the increased invoice price, the manufacturers were left with a substantial profit ranging from four-fifths of a cent to 1.2 cents per package.

At present (1930) the manufacturers are operating with the same tax and an invoice price reduced to $6.40 per thousand. This is from a dollar to a dollar and a half under the war level and probably means a decreased margin of profit per thousand. Offsetting this, however, is a tremendous increase in volume of production.

There is no assurance that the removal of the tax would benefit the farmer. That would depend upon how badly the

TABLE X

PRICES AND COSTS, SELECTED BRANDS OF CIGARETTES*
PER 1,000 CIGARETTES

	First six months of 1920	Ten months Ending Dec. 31, 1919
Brand No. 2		
Invoice price............................	$7.9398	$7.3453
Factory cost, including tax...............	5.9043	5.4626
Freight, selling, and advertising...........	.7122	.6123
Total Cost...........................	6.6165	6.0749
Leaf cost............................	2.1181	1.8615
Labor cost...........................	.1961	.1942
Net profit...........................	.3624	.4294
Brand No. 3		
Invoice price............................	7.9171	7.2984
Factory cost, including tax...............	5.6415	5.3442
Freight, selling and advertising............	.6374	.5917
Total cost...........................	6.2789	5.9359
Leaf cost............................	1.8301	1.5240
Labor cost...........................	.1770	.2121
Net profit...........................	.6759	.4968

(*) *The Tobacco Industry*, Federal Trade Commission, 1920, p. 31.

manufacturers wished to lower retail prices, or increase their profits and discounts without lowering prices.

To review the possibilities of what might happen in the event of the straight reduction of the tobacco tax, there are the following alternatives:

(1) The retail price might be lowered. This is a likely result because the discounts could be arranged in such a way that the purchasers of carton lots would get a better price and chain stores could cut some odd cents from the price. The figures in Table IX and Diagram III indicate that the tax increases in the past have been absorbed, to a large ex-

tent, by the companies while they continually lowered invoice prices, which is the policy to be expected of a semi-monopolistic group seeking to increase sales. A tax decrease would only enable them still further to develop their policy of attaining volume by slightly decreasing invoice price.

(2) The manufacturer's profit might be increased. The above table showed that profits were, to some extent, decreased in 1919 and 1920 when the deflated tax remained stationary and increases in costs forged ahead of increases in retail price. However, by 1921, the costs had deflated, especially leaf costs, and profits, under the present high tax, are higher than those under a low tax in 1916. (See Chapter III.) Any decrease in tax, therefore, would merely relieve the manufacturers of absorbing as much tax as they now absorb. Under monopoly conditions the prices are likely to be fixed at a point to yield the maximum profit regardless of the tax. Consequently, tax reduction would mean that, aside from small amounts which might be taken from invoice price, the amount of reduction would be pocketed by the manufacturer.

(3) The release of the pressure of the tax might result in slight increases in the prices paid to farmers for raw tobacco. This is unlikely. The figures in Table IX indicate the farmer got a larger deflated price per pound in 1919 with a high deflated tax, than in 1916 with a low tax, and that in 1922, when the tax had increased still more, the farm price had not dropped to pre-war levels. The basis for this conclusion will be more apparent in the later discussion of the factors controlling farm price. In these chapters it is apparent that supply is the main controlling factor, and that

buying, as they do, under practical monopoly conditions, the tobacco manufacturers offer only such prices as will cause the farmers to continue to produce what they need. Another reason why a permanent increase in farm price would be unlikely will appear from the discussion of the factors controlling production, in which it is evident that production is very sensitive to price, and slight increases in price lead to rapid expansion of supply with subsequent breaks in price.

It should be pointed out, however, that tobacco is practically the only commodity still bearing a wartime burden. Amusement and automobile taxes have been wholly abolished and the income tax reduced. There would seem to be no good reason why tobacco, which is produced and manufactured in so small a section of the country, should continue to bear a war burden, except the long-standing habit of the nation of depending to such a large extent upon tobacco for its revenue, and the ease of administering the tax. The argument for some adjustment of this tax is strengthened by the fact that the increased volume of production is increasing the amount of the government revenue by leaps and bounds, the income from this source having doubled since 1920.

BURDEN ON SMALL INCOMES

The extent to which the tobacco tax is regressive is apparent when it is realized that it amounts to over $3.00 per capita and is paid out of small as well as large budgets. Smoking is now so universal that tobacco is no longer in the class of luxuries. A recent study of the budgets of Negro tenant farmers in Georgia (probably the lowest income group in the country) showed that they spent about $18.00 annually or six per cent of their cash income for tobacco. And of this, about $3.50 was tax.[1]

Certainly it can be maintained that in any industry which contributes as much to the Government as does the tobacco industry, it is the moral obligation of the Government to do all in its power to see that all contributors to the industry receive a fair share. As it is, however, the Government is not in a position to materially offset tobacco price; and if it were, increase in price would lead to over-production.

PROPOSED ADJUSTMENT FOR FARM RELIEF

A way has, however, been suggested by Dr. Clarence Heer of the University of North Carolina, by which the tax should be so modified that the producers could receive at least indirect benefits from the change. This proposal is that the Federal Government, following the principle applied to the inheritance tax, rebate to the tobacco growing states an amount equal to an excise tax levied by the state on the sales of raw tobacco. The levy of such an excise, to be rebated from the Federal Tax, would not change the amount of that tax but would merely redistribute a portion of it to the tobacco growing states. Thus the farmers of the tobacco growing states would at least have the benefit of reduced local taxation and of improved roads and schools, while the tax paid by the retail purchaser would not be increased but merely divided between the Federal Government and the states.

A reduction of somewhat under $100,000,000 in the Federal Tax (less than one-fourth) would reduce the total

[1] This assumes that these low income farmers used cheap grades of smoking and chewing tobacco rather than manufactured cigarettes. The proportion of tax to purchase price of manufactured cigarettes is higher.

Federal revenues by hardly three per cent and could as easily be spared as the previous reductions in the income, corporation, and automobile taxes. Such a reduction would be brought about by the levy of an excise by the tobacco growing states of about 12½ cents per pound upon the sale of raw tobacco for domestic consumption, this amount to be reimbursed to the state from internal revenues now collected, just as inheritance taxes levied by a state are returned from Federal inheritance taxes. This would mean a state revenue as shown in Table XI.

TABLE XI

Amounts Resulting from Excise Tax of 12½ Cents* Per Pound on Sales of Tobacco

(Figured conservatively on the basis of 1927 crop)

North Carolina	$32,350,000
Kentucky	12,786,666
Virginia	8,100,000
South Carolina	5,060,000
Tennessee	4,520,000
Georgia	3,800,000
Pennsylvania	3,000,000
Wisconsin	2,000,000
Connecticut	1,926,666
Ohio	1,680,000

* 12½ cents on domestic consumption is equivalent to about 6¼ cents on the total crop, since half this crop is exported and would have to be tax exempt.

SUMMARY

The tobacco tax amounts to over four hundred million dollars, twelve per cent of the income of the United States. Cigarette taxes make up three-fourths of this. Since the war, cigarettes taxes have not decreased. When considered in relation to the cost of living they have actually increased. Since desire for volume sales tends to hold retail price down there is no assurance that a reduction of the tax would benefit the farmer in any way because it would probably be passed on to the smoker, and such reduction is not particularly needed by the smoker. However, a division of part of this revenue among the tobacco producing states by the device of a state excise tax rebated from the Federal Tax would be of indirect benefit to the grower through reductions in his local taxes.

CHAPTER VI

CONSUMPTION AND FARM PRICE

THE DEMAND for flue-cured tobacco is difficult to determine since it is partially used for domestic manufacture and partially exported. That part which is manufactured in the United States is blended in various ways with other tobaccos in the manufacture of cigarettes, pipe, and chewing tobacco. Cigarettes are the most accurate, but not exact, index of this demand, for about sixty per cent of flue-cured tobacco manufactured in the United States is used for cigarettes and about seventy-five per cent of the tobacco in domestic cigarettes is flue-cured.

The present complete distribution of flue-cured is about as follows: forty-eight per cent exported; thirty per cent used in domestic cigarettes; twenty-two per cent in smoking and plug tobacco. The figures are not available to make this more than a very general estimate.

RAPID INCREASE IN CONSUMPTION

The close association with cigarettes is the reason for the rapidly increasing consumption. Diagram I, Chapter I, showed the rapid increase of flue-cured production from about thirty per cent of all chewing, smoking, and export types to about sixty per cent.

Table XII and Diagram IV show the increase in tobacco used for the domestic manufacture of cigarettes, the increase in exports of all leaf tobacco, and the level trend of other tobacco products.

Up to 1921, and especially during the war, the exports of leaf were far ahead of the amount used in domestic manufacture of cigarettes. Since 1921, however, the domestic manufacture has rapidly overhauled exports.

The trend in leaf used for the domestic manufacture of cigarettes is continually up with few recessions.[1] This sharply upward trend in the demand indicates that the manufacturers have not yet reached the point of diminishing returns in the expenditure of money for advertising and the acquisition of new women smokers. The slackening of either of these factors would mean that the demand trend would cease to climb so sharply and begin to flatten out into a parabola.

It is especially worthy of note that the post-war deflation in industry caused only a momentary halt in the upward

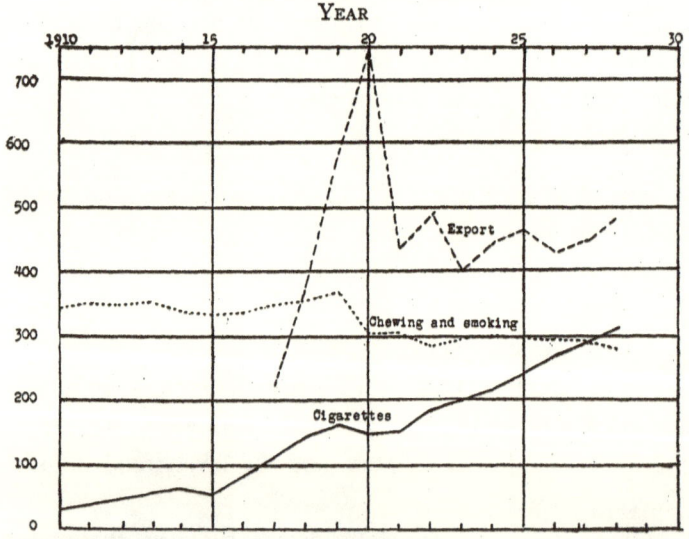

DIAGRAM IV
LEAF TOBACCO USED IN CIGARETTES, IN OTHER NON-CIGAR PRODUCTS AND LEAF EXPORTED, UNIT MILLION LBS.

[1] Fitted through average poundage and mid year as zero point. The equation of this trend, since 1915, omitting the war years, is increase in leaf $(y) = 26.17$ times increase in years. (x)

TABLE XII
LEAF TOBACCO USED IN MANUFACTURE OF CIGARETTES* AND SMALL CIGARETTES MANUFACTURED IN CALENDAR YEAR

Calendar Year	Leaf tobacco used in the manufacture of small cigarettes calendar year Million Pounds	Small cigarettes manufactured calendar year Billions
1928	310	109
1927	290	100
1926	267	92
1925	244	82
1924	218	73
1923	200	67
1922	169	56
1921	153	52
1920	147	47
1919	167	53
1918	146	47
1917	113	35
1916	78	25
1915	56	18
1914	62	17
1913	56	16
1912	47	13
1911	38	10
1910	31	9

*See appendix for conversion factor.

swing of cigarettes and, after a slight drop in 1920, the climb was immediately renewed. War and women have held the increment of cigarette sales steady since 1921.

Even the depression of 1929-1930 failed to halt the upward trend of cigarette demand as reports for 1930 indicate a slight increase in sales over 1929.

Of course this increment cannot continue indefinitely. The 1928 output amounted to over a hundred million packages of twenty cigarettes each week. Figured on the basis of adults over fifteen years of age, this is nearly a package and a half a week for every man and woman, without allowance for those who may prefer cigars, pipes, or chewing tobacco. There is evidently a limit to this rapid increase. When that limit is reached it may be expected that the trend of demand for tobacco will increase only in proportion to the population. The time needed to reach the limit of saturation will depend upon the extent to which smokers who now use cigars or pipe are converted to cigarettes, and the acquisition by non-smokers, of the cigarette habit.

The slight fluctuations of consumption around its trend and the steadiness of the climb indicate a demand which continues to increase and would probably be very resistant to increases in retail price. This peculiarity of the relation of demand to retail selling price arises from the fact that tobacco is habit-forming. The large increases in demand come from new proselytes to the habit rather than from increases in consumption by old users; and once the habit is formed, slight changes in the small retail price would make little difference to the habituated. Thus the price policy of the manufacturer is controlled not so much by the necessity of holding old customers as of acquiring new ones.

Little need be said of the export requirements except that, with the exception of a rise during the war and a deflation in 1920, they have been fairly steady. The exports of flue-cured have kept slightly ahead of the domestic consumption for cigarettes.

The consumption of flue-cured for the manufacture of chewing and smoking tobacco is also very steady. Diagram IV shows that the amount of leaf used for this purpose has practically no trend and small fluctuations. Of this leaf used for chewing and smoking mixtures only about 45 per cent is flue-cured. Its small fluctuations, therefore, do not materially affect the total fluctuation in requirements for manufacture. The fluctuation in these requirements for flue-cured tobacco is largely governed by the fluctuation in requirements for cigarettes.

LEAF USED FOR CIGARETTES AND FARM PRICE

The relation of consumption to farm price paid for raw tobacco can best be understood by recurring to the monopoly conditions of buying described in Chapters III and IV. Under these circumstances the companies would not be expected to bid higher prices for tobacco than would be necessary to cause the farmers to raise enough to fill the manufacturers' needs and not shift to other crops. This is about the situation revealed by the statistics. The long-time trends of consumption and price are almost unrelated. And the trend in price since 1913 by no means keeps pace with the rapid climb of consumption. These trends are shown in Diagram

DIAGRAM V
LEAF TOBACCO USED IN MANUFACTURE OF CIGARETTES AND DEFLATED NORTH CAROLINA PRICE

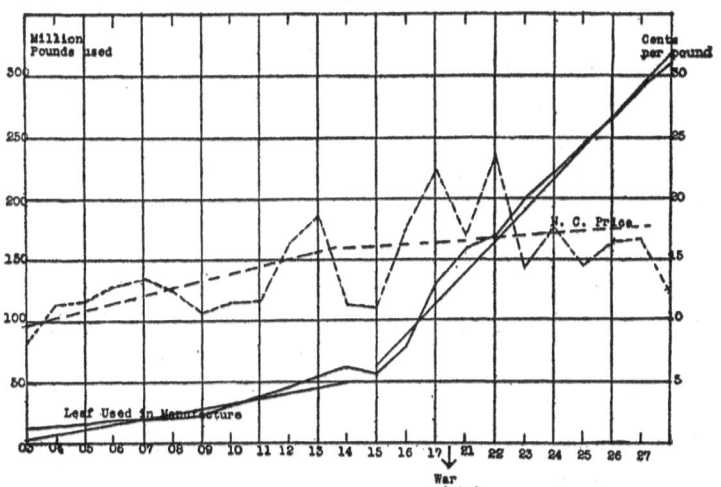

V presenting the consumption of leaf tobacco in cigarettes and the deflated North Carolina price.

If, as is ordinarily true, the price increased with the demand, one would expect a positive correlation between the increases in price and increases in amount taken. Such, however, is not the case. The coefficient obtained by correlating the annual changes in price and consumption for cigarette manufacture from 1903 to 1928 is only—.014 which is indeterminate.[3]

TABLE XIII

NORTH CAROLINA PRICE AND TOTAL SUPPLY AND DISAPPEARANCE OF FLUE-CURED TOBACCO, 1917 TO 1927. (MILLION POUNDS)

Year	Production	Stocks July 1	Total supply July 1	Disappearance year commencing July 1	Ratio of N. Carolina price to cost of living
1929	764	590	1353	754	11.8
1928	740	565	1305	715	12.5
1927	716	466	1182	617	14.6
1926	564	455	1020	553	16.4
1925	576	462	1039	583	14.6
1924	437	477	913	451	17.6
1923	593	439	1032	555	14.4
1922	409	441	849	411	21.4
1921	371	483	855	414	17.0
1920	631	304	935	452	12.3
1919	487	327	815	511	28.8
1918	487	292	779	452	20.9
1917	359	253	612	320	22.3

DISAPPEARANCE AND PRICE

But there is another index of demand. If, instead of using the consumption in the manufacture of cigarettes, we

[3] This coefficient figured on annual changes. To be sure no material error occurred through correlating only cigarette requirements, these requirements were combined with the smoking and plug requirements by weighting cigarettes 1½ times the chewing and smoking weight, which is roughly the proportion of flue-cured taken for each. This weighted series, correlated with price, gave a coefficient of —.236.

CONSUMPTION AND FARM PRICE 73

use the disappearance of flue-cured tobacco, we obtain another statistical test. The disappearance of flue-cured is calculated by taking the stocks on hand July 1, adding the current crop, and subtracting the stock on hand on the subsequent July 1. This gives the domestic disappearance plus the total exported but does not take into account what may

DIAGRAM VI
NORTH CAROLINA DEFLATED PRICE AND DISAPPEARANCE OF FLUE-CURED TOBACCO. UNIT 1 CENT PRICE, 10 MILLION LBS. DISAPPEARANCE
TREND PRICE $y = -.86x$
DISAPPEARANCE $y = 27.3x$

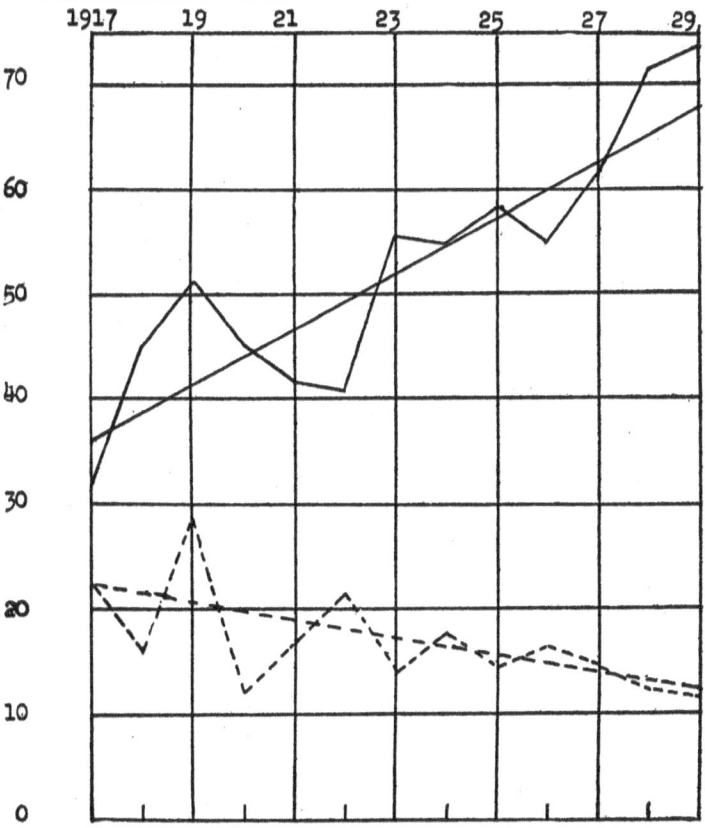

74   THE PLIGHT OF CIGARETTE TOBACCO

have been placed in storage abroad after having been exported.[4]

Table XIII gives the supply and disappearance of flue-cured tobacco and Diagram VI shows this in relation to price.[5]

Thus by both tests the demand and farm price of tobacco are practically unrelated. Price merely inflates enough to keep the farmer raising sufficient tobacco for the trade. As we shall see in the succeeding chapter, price is much more closely related to the supply in sight than it is to the consumption, which is what would be expected under conditions of monopoly buying. From this diagram it is apparent that since 1917 neither the long-time trends nor the annual fluctuations of price and disappearance show any correspondence.

[4] The British stocks of flue-cured in storage are about equal to the poundage exported annually.

[5] The correlation between deviations of disappearance from its trend and the deviations of price from its trend is only —.030.

CHAPTER VII

PRODUCTION AND FARM PRICE

THE MOST outstanding peculiarity of the supply of tobacco is the tremendous carry-over of stock from year to year. For practically all uses tobacco is aged from twelve to twenty-four months, usually about eighteen, before manufacture.

STORED STOCKS

From the auction market floor it goes to be redried and then into large hogsheads which are placed in well-ventilated warehouses for aging. This process of holding tobacco in storage keeps a large proportion of the capital of the manufacturers tied up in inventories, but it also puts them in a very independent market position since they have three times the annual domestic consumption in storage. This also enables them to average their cost of leaf over three years' crops and be relieved of embarrassment from violent fluctuations in single years. It also means that they are under no immediate pressure to buy the current offerings of the farmers.

Diagram VII and Table XIV show the increase of flue-cured tobacco in storage and of all tobacco held on January first of each successive year.

While the total of non-cigar types in storage has increased from seven hundred and fifty million to over fifteen hundred million, the flue-cured in storage has increased from three hundred and thirty million to seven hundred and ninety million. Thus in ten years the proportion of flue-cured of the total in storage has increased from forty per cent to over fifty

TABLE XIV
STOCKS OF LEAF TOBACCO
(Reported by Manufacturers January 1)* Million Pounds

Year	All non-cigar types	Flue-cured	Pounds used domestic manufacture non-cigar types (†)
1929	1373	766	...
1928	1520	756	587
1927	1416	629	574
1926	1385	603	560
1925	1266	579	543
1924	1220	620	516
1923	1068	544	502
1922	1174	570	467
1921	1061	524	438
1920	962	449	453
1919	913	427	474
1918	893	429	526
1917	758	332	473

(*) Excludes stocks of small manufacturers and stocks in hands of farmers and in bonded warehouses.
(†) As revised with Bureau of Internal Revenue conversion factor, see Appendix.

per cent. All types and flue-cured have increased faster than the domestic requirements for the manufacture of cigarettes, and chewing, smoking, and snuff products. See Diagram VII.

DIAGRAM VII
RATE OF INCREASE IN STOCK OF CHEWING, SMOKING AND EXPORT AND OF FLUE-CURED STOCKS AND OF DOMESTIC REQUIREMENTS FOR NON-CIGAR MANUFACTURE IN HUNDRED MILLION POUNDS

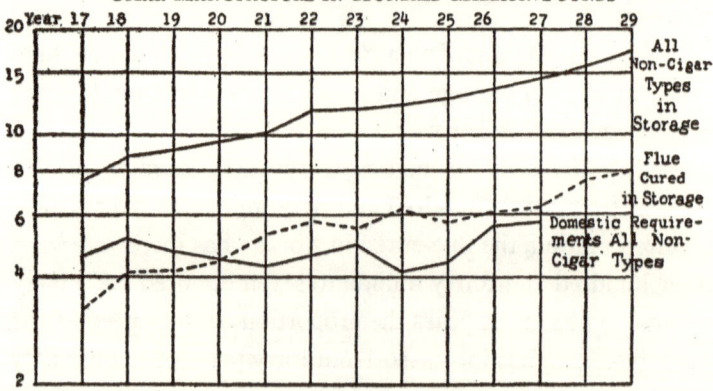

The stored stock of flue-cured alone is now greater than the total domestic requirements for all non-cigar types and the stored stock of all non-cigar types is about three times the annual domestic requirements for these types. This great amount in storage renders fluctuation in annual production less important in determining prices than the fluctuations of commodities where the stored stock is not so large.

TREND OF PRODUCTION AND CONSUMPTION

The rapid increase in stocks would indicate an overproduction which has gone into the warehouses of the manufacturers at cheap prices. Since, however, flue-cured is

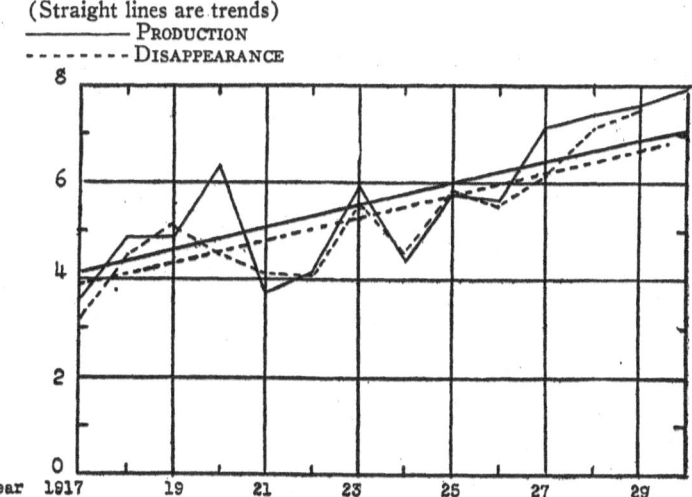

DIAGRAM VIII
PRODUCTION AND DISAPPEARANCE OF FLUE-CURED TOBACCO IN HUNDRED MILLION POUNDS
(Straight lines are trends)
——— PRODUCTION
- - - - - - - DISAPPEARANCE

mixed in manufacture with other types and since part of the crop is exported, its over-production can only be gauged by the rate of increase in the disappearance of flue-cured stocks. Diagram VIII presents these two curves. It will be observed that they rise together, with production keeping slightly ahead of disappearance during most years and going markedly ahead every few years. This over-production was especially marked in 1927, 1928, and 1929. It was in these three years that the rapid increase of flue-cured tobacco in storage took place.

However, when it is considered that the manufacturers are not buying to meet their present requirements, but the requirements of two or three years hence, and that these requirements, as far as the cigarette types are concerned, are constantly increasing, it will be seen that production must be gauged not so much on present takings but on the probable expansion of takings in the next two years. From this angle it would appear that while occasional production of more than the current requirements has been building up the stocks in storage, the rate of increase in production has not been sufficiently rapid to discount future increases in consumption should they continue as in the past twelve years.[1]

AREAS OF INCREASED PRODUCTION

As to the localities of increase in production there are two: Georgia has, since 1918, become a producer of flue-cured tobacco and now produces nearly a hundred million pounds annually. The area in Georgia, now devoted to tobacco, was formerly a sea island cotton area. This latter crop was ruined by the boll weevil and the destitute farmers had to cast about for a new use for their land and labor.

[1] The trend of increase in production through an average of 548 was 26.69. In disappearance the trend through an average of 523 was 27.3. See Diagram VIII.

PRODUCTION AND FARM PRICE

DIAGRAM IX
PRICES OF FLUE-CURED TOBACCO IN GEORGIA AND IN THE NORTH CAROLINA NEW BELT

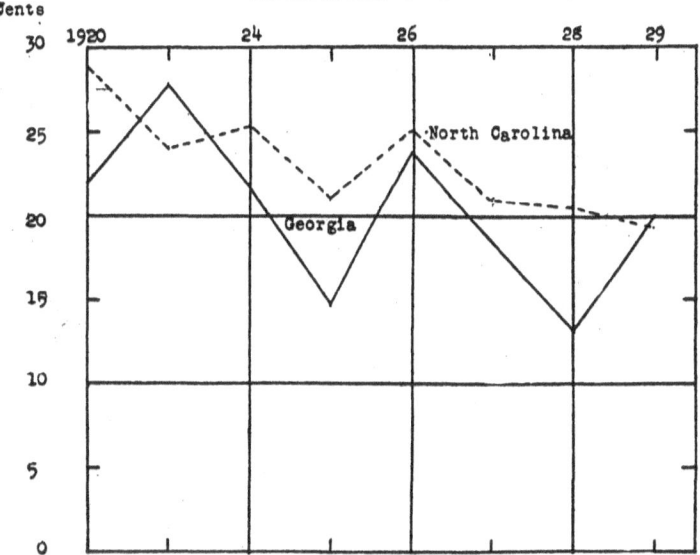

Under the stimulus of the State College of Agriculture and the A. B. and A. Railroad, flue-cured tobacco was tried, and proved remarkably successful, the quality comparing favorably with that of North Carolina. The result was the expansion of tobacco culture into all the counties which formerly grew sea island cotton.

The tobacco companies have been accused of artificially fostering this Georgia expansion by shading up the Georgia prices. The statistics of price do not bear this out. Diagram IX shows that Georgia price runs continually under North Carolina price.

The true situation was this: When Georgia farmers began to produce tobacco in 1918, 1919, and 1920, war prices were prevailing and they found a bonanza use for lands

THE PLIGHT OF CIGARETTE TOBACCO

which the boll weevil had ruined. Even after the war, tobacco did not deflate as rapidly as cotton so they could still raise tobacco more profitably at current prices. Under these circumstances it was not necessary for the companies

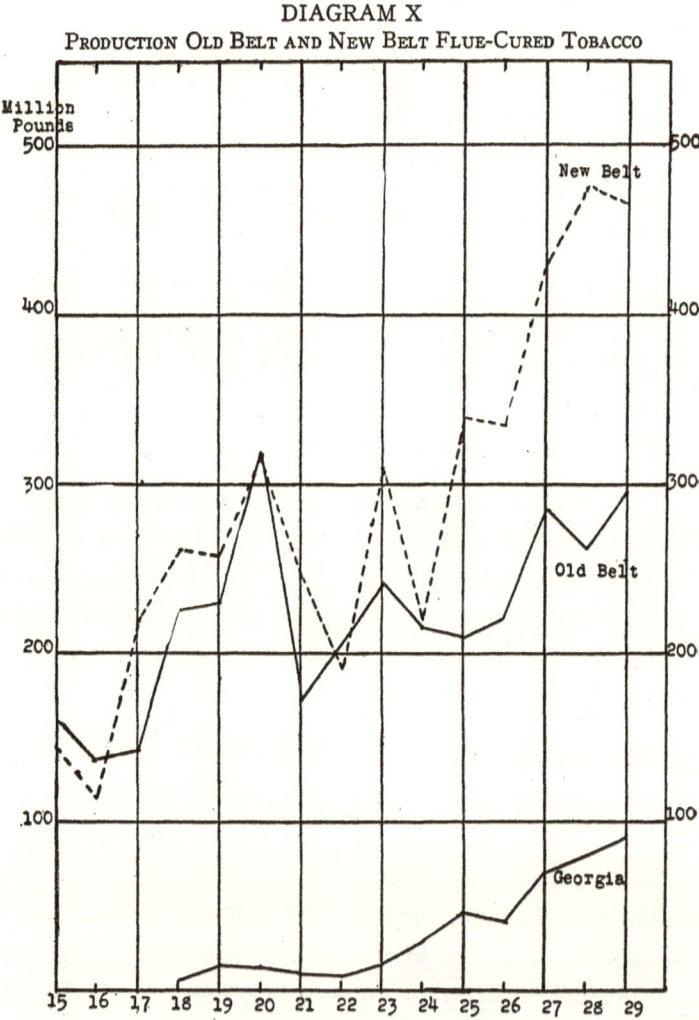

DIAGRAM X
PRODUCTION OLD BELT AND NEW BELT FLUE-CURED TOBACCO

to stimulate production artificially. The factors in the situation were such as to promote a rapid expansion without this aid.

The second area of rapid expansion of production is in North Carolina and South Carolina, mostly in the area known as the new belt. Diagram X shows that the old belt (see Map I) has increased production only slightly while the new belt including Georgia has expanded rapidly. Unlike the expansion in Georgia, this North Carolina overproduction does not come about through substitution of cotton for tobacco as cotton acreage has also increased in eastern North Carolina.

The reason why tobacco has gained favor in areas where it may be substituted for cotton is apparent from Diagram XI showing the purchasing power of an acre of cotton and an acre of tobacco. From this it is apparent that the per acre value of tobacco, low as it is, is higher in comparison to the 1910-14 level than is the value of an acre of cotton. It is also apparent from this diagram that the depressions in cotton, which have numbered four since 1910, are more violent than the corresponding depressions in tobacco. In expanding tobacco acreage the farmer is, therefore, choosing the lesser of two evils.

DIAGRAM XI
INDEX OF PURCHASING POWER OF AN ACRE OF COTTON AND AN ACRE OF TOBACCO BASE 1910-1914 = 100%

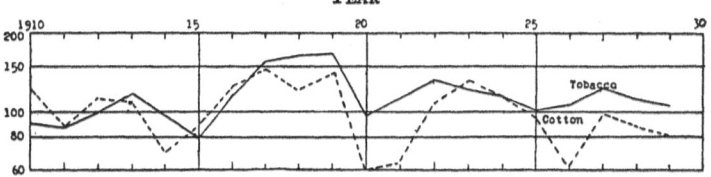

CHANGES IN FARM PRICE AND PRODUCTION

The reaction of farm price and production is mutual. This year's price affects next year's production and this year's production affects this year's price. We shall analyse these two actions separately.

Tobacco production is very sensitive to increases in farm price. The relationship between general tobacco price and production and cotton price and production is given in Diagram XII which shows that the two crops follow the same general law. Both show tremendous increases in production the year after the farmer's per acre value increases, and decreases in production following price decreases.[2] This relationship for flue-cured is indexed by North Carolina price and production as shown in Diagram XIII. In this diagram the close correspondence between price one year and production the next is evident. The size of the price and production fluctuations are also worthy of note.[3] The warning here for

DIAGRAM XII A.
INDEX PER ACRE VALUE OF COTTON AND PRODUCTION FOLLOWING YEAR
BASE 1910-1914 = 100%

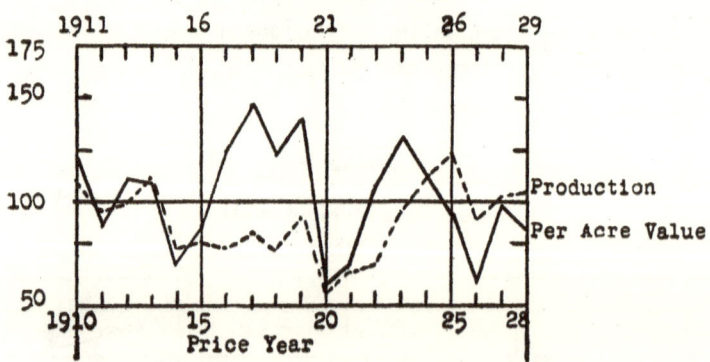

[2] The correlation for both cotton and tobacco is over .7.
[3] The correlation between price one year and production the next is over .9 with small probable error.

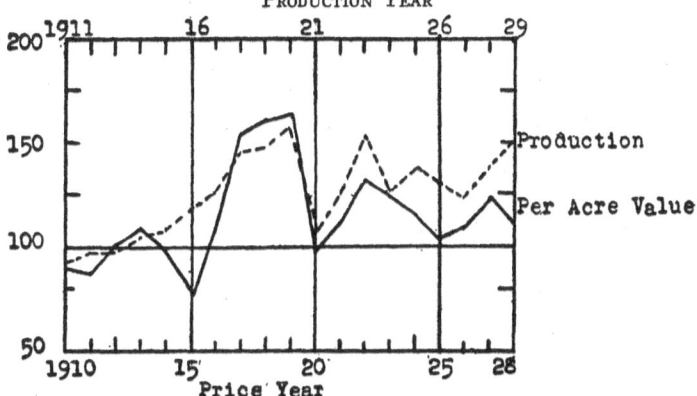

DIAGRAM XII B.
INDEX PER ACRE VALUE OF TOBACCO AND PRODUCTION FOLLOWING YEAR
BASE 1910-1914 = 100%

a coöperative association or any organization aiming to improve farm price is that such improvement will defeat itself unless closely allied to efforts to control production. It is of small advantage to raise the price one year merely to have that act as a bait to tempt thousands of farmers to expand tobacco acreage and break the price by flooding the market the following year.

INCREASE OF SUPPLY AND PRICE

The second reaction of production on the same year's price is not so marked because, as has been pointed out, three times the annual requirements are in storage, and this large carry-over must be added to the current production to arrive at the total supply in sight.

However, when the relation of total supply in sight to price is calculated a high negative correlation is obtained. Diagram XIV and Table XIII (previous chapter) show this relation.[4]

[4] The correlation coefficient is —.578. Based on annual changes.

DIAGRAM XIII
North Carolina Price (Deflated) and Production Following Year.
Unit, Price 1 Cent, Production 10 Million lbs.

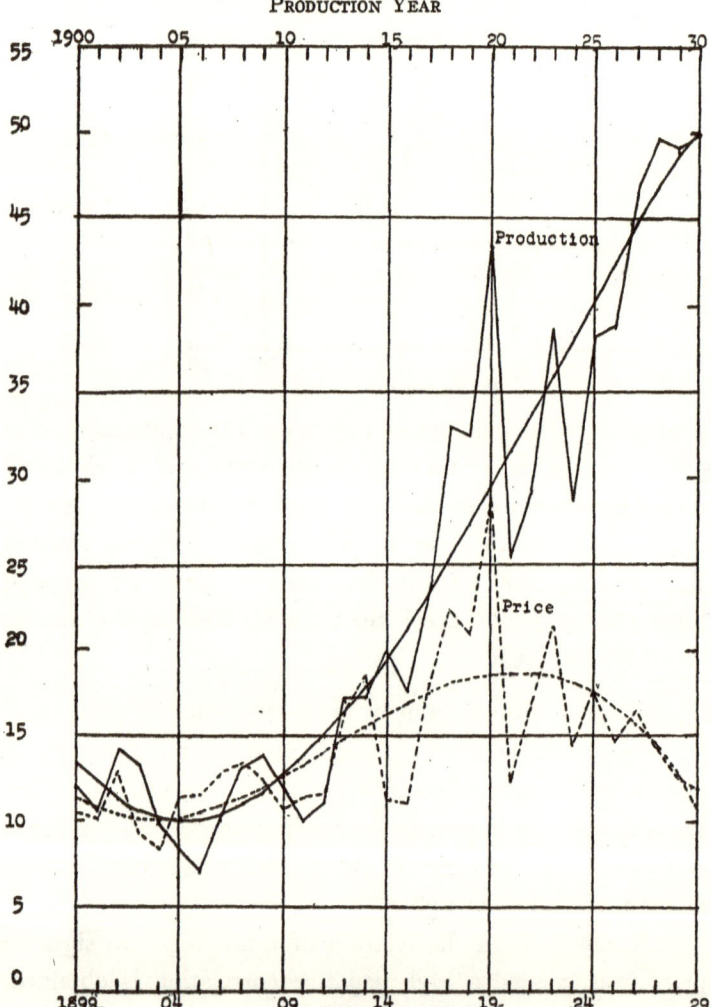

Trends: Price, $y = 16.17 + .675x - .0228x^2 - .0031x^3$
Production $y = 19.6 + 1.723x + .0531x^2 - .0021x^3$

DIAGRAM XIV
North Carolina Price and Supply of Flue-Cured Tobacco Price in Cents, Supply in Hundred Million Pounds
Year

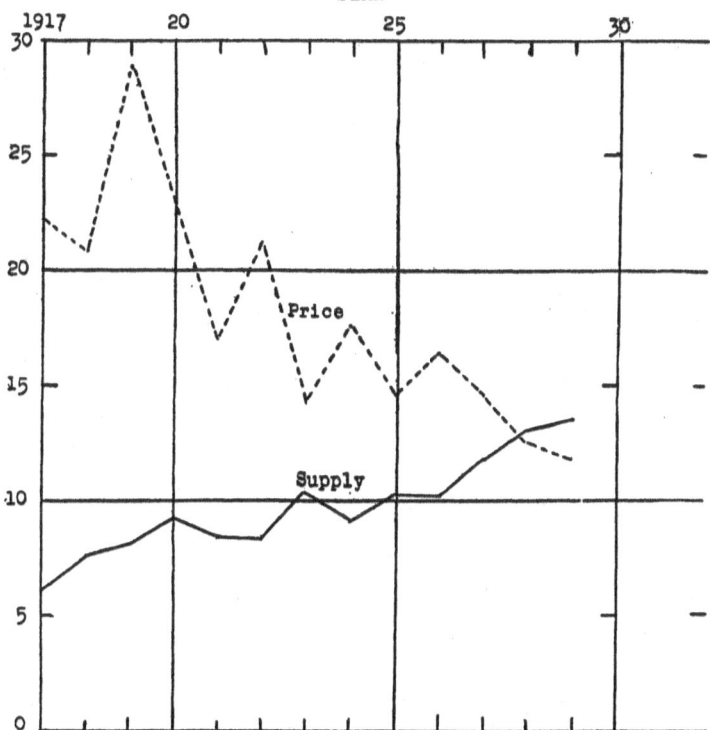

There are two factors which associate price strongly with supply. First the buyers will obviously bid less with a large supply in sight and second, as was pointed out in Chapter III, a large crop, if secured on the basis of large yields per acre, is likely to include an unusual proportion of low grade tobacco. Thus increased yields tend to have a doubly depressing effect on farm price.

In brief, the production of all leaf types and of flue-cured runs slightly ahead of consumption, increasing a little more rapidly. Over the past ten years this has augmented the stocks of manufacturers until they have three times the annual requirements in storage.

Production fluctuates violently responding immediately to changes in price so that marked price increases cause overproduction.

On the other hand, the fluctuation of supply in sight, i.e. the stocks on hand plus current production are closely associated with current prices. Since it was found in the previous chapter that consumption showed little relation to price it is evident that production is the dominant factor in determining farm price.

There is one other price factor which comes into play only occasionally, namely, the temper of the farmers. In 1910 the prices of burley tobacco fell so low that farmers decided to cease the cultivation of tobacco. Night riders scoured the country, burning the barns and scraping seed beds of those who persisted in attempting to make a crop. This was a very effective method of raising the price the following year.

Since that time the companies have been sensitive to farmers' complaints when they reached such a crescendo as to threaten real action. A similar period was witnessed in 1929 when two successive low priced crops caused indignation meetings, petitions to Congress, and some concrete talk about reduction of acreage. The response on the part of the companies was an increase in farm price all over the belt which, evidently from newspaper comment, put the farmers into a better frame of mind. In slang this process might be termed kidding the farm along. The actual price increase on the same grades of tobacco during this period on two markets were as follows:[5]

Week Ending	Smithfield, N. C.				South Hill, Virginia			
	Leaf	Cutters	Lugs	Total graded	Leaf	Cutters	Lugs	Total graded
Sept. 28..	15.51	21.90	12.83	15.75	Not open			
Oct. 5..	17.73	22.13	13.13	17.82	Not given			14.97
Oct. 12..	20.09	24.20	15.78	19.82	14.92	23.75	14.63	16.15
Oct. 19..	24.12	30.83	16.26	25.11	17.26	25.85	12.81	17.74
Oct. 26..	25.21	32.54	15.40	26.71				
Last two weeks of season...	21.94	27.65	14.81	22.55	14.55	37.07	11.01	17.65

There was not sufficient variation in the character or amount of the tobacco appearing to account for this price increase in any other way than the desire of the buyers to keep the farmers from cutting their acreage too radically the following year. However, it will be noted that prices eased off again before the close of the season.

This factor does not come into play very often for it is only in seasons of desperation that the farmers become vocal enough to threaten to unite. Nevertheless, this is one more indication of the powerful influence the companies have on price and their tendency to manipulate it, not in accordance with their immediate requirements, but in accordance with their long time requirements and with the nature of the supply in sight.

[5] From current reports of Tobacco Grading Service. U. S. Department of Agriculture.

CHAPTER VIII
SUMMARY

THE STRONG position of the manufacturer, the weak position of the farmer, the great reserve supply of stored tobacco, the tendency of the manufacturer to absorb any tax reductions or pass them on in reduced retail price, the fluctuation of farm price with supply, regardless of demand, and the general tendency of price to decline since 1920 regardless of the rapid increase in consumption—an increase more than equalled by the increase in production—and finally the tendency of the farmers to bring in an oversupply of tobacco after they have received encouragement in the form of slight price increases—all these picture the discouraging position of the producer of flue-cured tobacco.

However, great as these difficulties have proved, they are not insurmountable. If the producers of cigarette tobacco are to escape the conditions of a sweated industry developing rural slums, these difficulties must be surmounted by resolute action. After ten years of experience with coöperation in the South, and with the encouragement added by the financing of the Federal Farm Board, the friends of coöperation feel that a new coöperative movement, planned to eliminate some of the weaknesses of the former movement, would go far toward meeting the situation.

Probably the most beneficial development would come from the growth of a stronger spirit of coöperation between the manufacturer and the farmer—a realization of mutual interests. Such realization was present in the early days of the industry. When the Dukes began the manufacture of tobacco, they were, for a while, also producers of the raw material. As long as the industry was small there was a semi-personal relationship between the farmer and the manufacturer. But with the transition to large manufacturing corporations, the relationship became more remote, more impersonal. It was then that the present maladjustment in the distribution of tobacco grew up.

The consolidation phase of the industry was doubtless necessary. It made possible unprecedented economies in cigarette manufacture and selling. It ushered in advertising campaigns of increasing magnitude which have multiplied the consumption of cigarettes forty-fold in twenty years. All this has benefited the farmer in that this has made possible a great expansion in leaf tobacco production. However, the benefit has taken the form of allowing a greater number of farmers to grow tobacco at a low income, rather than increasing the income of each individual farmer. Reference to the ratio of the North Carolina price to the cost of living shown in Diagram XIII indicates that the real value per pound of tobacco in 1929 is about what it was in 1900 and lower than it has been since 1910. The per acre value shown in Diagram II shows the same trend. Thus, what share the farmer has had in the marvelous progress of the tobacco industry has been diffused among a number of new producers of tobacco rather than toward improving the lot of the individual farmer.

MUTUAL INTERESTS

Those who handle tobacco from the time of its sprouting to the time of its consumption have certain common interests. They are: (1) stability of the industry in all its phases; (2) improvement of the quality of the product; and (3) increase in the volume of out-put at a profitable price.

The Government, which gets half a billion dollars from the tobacco industry, should especially be aware of a moral obligation to insure as far as possible the equitable participation of all contributors to the industry. For this reason a modification of the tax was proposed so that some of the funds now going to the United States Treasury would be reallocated to the states, and the tobacco farmers be indirectly benefited by local tax reductions.

BENEFITS OF COÖPERATIVE MARKETING

From the viewpoint of the manufacturer, stability and improvement of quality are the chief benefits to be derived from the improvement of the position of the tobacco farmer. It is possible to conceive of such conditions as would lead to the cessation of production of tobacco by American farmers, in which case the tobacco manufacturers would suffer the same embarrassment which now confronts the rubber industry in its dependence for its raw materials on other nations. Should the farm price of tobacco remain depressed several factors could contribute to the curtailment of production. The rising standards of living might drive increasing numbers to the city. A recovery in cotton or the development of another profitable cash crop might lead to a wholesale substitution of these crops for tobacco. A real impetus to the movement toward diversification of crops might appreciably reduce the tobacco acreage per farm. These possibilities must be balanced against the possibility of the extension of tobacco acreage to new lands, the possibility of the further substitution of tobacco for cotton in the event of continued cotton depression, and the possibility of increases in yield per acre.

With so many factors present, the stabilization of the production of a crop as sensitive to price as tobacco is a difficult proposition. Hundreds of thousands of individual farmers must not only be educated to the advantages of acreage limitation but must also find profitable uses for the acres released by curtailment of tobacco cultivation. This is a slow process, but one which could be speeded up by an efficient and respected coöperative movement.

The improvement in quality depends largely upon the requirements of the manufacturers and exporters of high grade tobaccos. They are the only ones in possession of the knowledge of how much the production of the higher grades could be increased without destroying the premium in price which they now receive. It would seem, however, from the facts of consumption—the increase in amounts taken at a relatively steady retail price—that leaf prices could be improved, even to the extent of slight increases in retail price, without materially affecting the demand of the ultimate consumer of cigarettes. The semi-monopolistic policies of the companies could be relied upon to increase their output and maintain retail prices at the point of maximum profit to them.

From the viewpoint of the present movement to reëstablish coöperative marketing of tobacco, there are the following manifest advantages to the farmer:

(1) He secures a stronger market position through collective rather than individual bargaining.

(2) His tobacco is sold strictly by grade with assurance of the proper premiums for better quality.

(3) There is a possibility that after the preliminary experience has been passed, the costs of marketing would be reduced.

(4) With the passage of the recent Federal Farm Loan act, the farmer secures financial backing for coöperative movements which was not hitherto available.

The operations of the Federal Farm Board inject into the present situation an element totally lacking in the situation of the former Tri-State Tobacco Growers Association, namely the possibility of affecting the production credit dilemma by organizing credit corporations subsidiary to the coöperative. These credit corporations would have part of their capital stock advanced by the Federal Farm Board and part by local subscribers. Thus, with a relatively small local subscription, added to aid from the Farm Board, with these multiplied by the discounting power of the Federal Intermediate Credit Banks, an important new source of credit would be open to members of the association offsetting, to some extent, the evils of the present production credit situation as described in Chapter II.

(5) He would receive more accurate information as to market conditions and advice on controlling his operations so as to meet these conditions.

From the viewpoint of the manufacturer, as has been indicated, there are also potential benefits to be derived from a farmer's coöperative.

(1) They would buy strictly graded tobacco, rather than lots averaged by the snap judgment of buyers bidding on from one hundred to three hundred lots an hour.

(2) A coöperative of effective size would eventually al-

low a reduction in the buying force and possibly a reduction in warehousing costs.

(3) A coöperative emphasizing marketing service would improve the grade of the product.

(4) There is the possibility of the stabilization of production which would reduce the inventories of the manufacturers in stocks stored during years of excess production.

DIFFICULTIES OF COÖPERATIVE MARKETING

On the other hand associations would face the following difficulties which are very real, and which need to be accounted for in their organization.

(1) They would deal with a highly organized, small group of buyers. The well intrenched position of these buyers calls for diplomacy rather than aggressiveness.

(2) These buyers have a tremendous supply on hand which would have to be considered in the market policy of the association.

(3) Competition between auction warehouses and coöperative warehouses would again create friction.

(4) Sellers at auction would receive cash, coöperative sellers only part cash and part in participation certificates. As pointed out, however, the financing of the Federal Farm Board will probably provide larger and more prompt advances than were made by the former association.

(5) The re-drying problem would have to be solved.

(6) More effective methods of regulating production than any yet applied would have to be developed in order to off-set the tendency of farmers to glut the market after price increases. This, it may be said, is a pressing problem not especially for coöperatives, but for any movement de-

signed to improve the position of the tobacco farmer. If production can be held within any reasonable limits the marketing association can help by carrying over some of the surplus of large crops.

As far as the producer is concerned, the way out of the present situation is easily enough phrased in a formula but very difficult to translate into action. The formula is reduction of the acreage in the money crop and substitution of food and feed crops; effort to improve the quality of tobacco produced on this smaller acreage; organization for pooling tobacco and selling strictly by grade. The individual farmer raises the following objections to any such course of action:

If I reduce my tobacco acreage, what control have I over others who may increase theirs and thereby depress the price which I receive for a smaller crop? On the other hand, if I happen to strike a good year I can make enough out of high priced tobacco to buy my food and feed profitably. If I enter an organization and make sacrifices the farmer who stays out will get the benefit of any price increases my organization brings about, and, if the buyers indulge in discriminatory practices, he will be given more than I get in order to persuade him to remain outside the organization.

It is also true that the wide fluctuations in the quantity and quality of tobacco produced work to the disadvantage of the manufacturers, and the resulting fluctuations in price keep the farmer hostile to the buyer. However, the manufacturer says to himself—it may be true that I would benefit by stabilization but I am getting along very well under the present system of buying at as low a figure as possible and raising the price occasionally when production falls off too sharply. Anyway, what is there to assure me that I will not

SUMMARY

be held up if the farmer's organizations gain too much power?

It is a long step from the system as it works in America to that in France where the Government Régie tells the farmer at the beginning of the season how much he can sell and how much he will be paid for it. American individualism will probably not give way to such a scheme. However, it would seem that there are advantages to both the manufacturer and the farmer in coöperating, possibly with government supervision, to endeavor to stabilize the production of the commodity along such a trend as to secure the quantity and grades demanded at a price to the farmer, which will give him a good wage for his labor and return on his capital, and insure the permanent position of tobacco production as a profitable branch of domestic agriculture.

APPENDIX A

THE following comments and safeguards need to be made regarding tobacco statistics. The basic data are all to be found in the Bulletin entitled *Stocks of Leaf Tobacco* published annually. This was formerly a publication of the Census Bureau. Now it is issued by the Bureau of Agricultural Economics. It contains the following items:

1. *Stocks of leaf tobacco on hand (quarterly)*. Only the large dealers come under the scope of the law requiring stock reports. Hence these figures exclude the small total stock in the hands of small dealers and in bonded warehouses. There is, however, practically no cigarette tobacco in the hands of small manufacturers. On the other hand a large proportion of the tobacco in bonded warehouses is cigarette tobacco. This is not a serious omission. They also exclude stocks in the hands of farmers. Except during the marketing season this also is an unimportant omission, because by December 1 nearly all the current crop has been marketed and by April 1 all markets are closed. No allowance is made for tobacco damaged by fire or water and the weight reported is the weight at which tobacco was purchased, without allowance for shrinkage. Recently manufacturers have been required to report stocks by grade.

2. *Acreage*. The acreage figures are those estimated by the Bureau of Agricultural Economics and share the same weaknesses as other crop estimates. They are however reliable in their large general fluctuations.

3. *Price*. The prices are December 1 prices. Season averages were formerly used by the Bureau of Agricultural Economics. But the problem of weight was so complicated

APPENDIX A

that they changed to December 1 prices. These obviously do not represent the true season's price but it has been found that the fluctuations in December 1 price follow closely the general fluctuations in price. The price of tobacco by types was not calculated before 1918 and for that reason longer time series by types are not available. Before 1918, however, price averages are given by states. For that reason North Carolina price has been used when a time series goes back of 1918. North Carolina raises only flue-cured tobacco and raises the great bulk of that crop. The price for that state is therefore highly accurate in indicating flue-cured price. Virginia, on the other hand, raises two other types besides flue-cured and the proportions of the flue-cured crop produced in Georgia and South Carolina are too small and are marketed too early in the season to warrant the use of their prices. The fluctuations in these states, however, generally follow the North Carolina fluctuations.

Price deflation. The retail index of the Bureau of Labor Statistics is used for deflation because this is available for a number of years back. Per acre values are deflated with the Bureau of Agricultural Economics index of prices paid by farmers which is the retail index exclusive of agricultural commodities.

Per Acre Value and Yield Per Acre. These are calculated from the Bureau of Agricultural Economics figures on acreage (see above), price (see above) and total production. (See next).

Total Production is based on the amounts of tobacco reported sold at the warehouses and is fairly accurate.

Tax Paid. This is a highly accurate figure reprinted in *Stocks of Leaf Tobacco* from reports of the Commissioner of Internal Revenue. Revenue figures follow closely the consumption figures. These are for the fiscal year. All others are for the calendar year.

Pounds of Leaf Tobacco Used in Manufacture. The data under this head represent the equivalent in unstemmed leaf tobacco of the quantities of the different kinds of tobacco apparently used by manufacturers. Stemmed leaf tobacco and scraps, cuttings and clippings are converted to equivalent in unstemmed leaf tobacco by the Bureau of Internal Revenue applying a conversion factor, that is, by dividing the quantities of stemmed or scraps, etc., by 3 and multiplying the quotient by 4. Prior to 1922 the conversion factor was division by 6 and multiplication by 10, etc. Therefore, the series as published in *Stocks of Leaf Tobacco* must be corrected for comparability.

Imports and Exports. Highly accurate figures from the Bureau of Foreign and Domestic Commerce.

The following balance sheet published in *Stocks of Leaf Tobacco* indicates the nature of all the above figures except prices and revenues:

APPENDIX A

Supply	1926 Pounds
Total (*)	3,211,620,146
Stocks held at beginning of year—total (*)	1,818,564,398
By manufacturers within the scope of the law and by dealers	1,747,172,474
In United States bonded warehouses	71,391,924
Production	1,297,889,000
Imports (gross)	67,905,655
Shipments from noncontiguous territories	27,261,093
Hawaii	....
Porto Rico	27,261,093
To balance distribution	....
Distribution	
Total (*)	3,211,620,146
Exported	479,931,771
Domestic	478,772,691
Foreign	1,159,080
Consumed	731,616,590
In registered factories	712,557,354
In bonded manufacturing warehouses	19,059,236
Shipments to noncontiguous territories	4,258,658
Alaska	1,364
Hawaii	10,134
Porto Rico	4,247,160
Stocks held at end of year—total(*)	1,841,645,426
By manufacturers within the scope of the law and by dealers	1,777,652,644
In United States bonded warehouses	63,992,782
To balance supply	154,167,701

*Not including stocks held by small manufacturers and by growers.

It will be noted from the last item "To balance supply" that the balance is out about three per cent owing to the omissions involved above, viz, omission from stocks of the amount stored by small manufacturers and growers, and omission of amounts consumed in bonded warehouses.

www.ingramcontent.com/pod-product-compliance
Lightning Source LLC
Chambersburg PA
CBHW030118010526
44116CB00005B/307